New STANDARD COURSE
Pitman Shorthand

New
STANDARD COURSE

Pitman Shorthand

Revised and Enlarged Edition

Pitman Publishing Corporation

New York   *Chicago*

Copyright 1936
PITMAN PUBLISHING CORPORATION
Printed in the United States of America

Preface

Isaac Pitman published the first edition of his shorthand system in 1837, and this revised and enlarged edition of the *New Standard Course in Pitman Shorthand* is issued to mark the centennial of the publication of the system.

History clearly shows that Isaac Pitman's invention has been the greatest contribution to the art of shorthand writing that the world has ever known. Millions of texts of the system have been purchased, and millions have used the system as a means of earning a livelihood. Today, one hundred years after its invention, it is continuously demonstrated that Isaac Pitman designed a writing instrument which meets the most exacting requirements of the stenographic art. The system stands without an equal for the swift and legible recording of speech. Almost without exception, the reporters of Congresses, Parliaments, Courts, throughout the English speaking world—wherever accurate recording of the proceedings is essential—use Pitmanic shorthand.

DISTINCTIVE FEATURES OF THE SYSTEM

Isaac Pitman published the system after an exhaustive study of the structure of the English language, and the system is the result of his scholarly and scientific analysis. Systems before Pitman, and even systems in use today depend largely upon the memorization of hundreds of special forms and arbitrary abbreviations due to the construction of their underlying principles. In Pitman Shorthand stress is placed upon the rational application of the principles used to represent the sounds occurring in English words, and it may be said that Isaac Pitman turned shorthand writing from an art into a science. Several generations of expert writers and teachers have built improvements upon the foundation laid by Isaac Pitman, with the result that today the Pitman writer knows that the system he uses is an instrument in which he may place the greatest confidence.

Handwriting Motion Inadequate. The consonants of the language are represented by a series of simple strokes, selected to provide the most facile joinings with each other. Because these strokes do not follow the slope of ordinary longhand writing, they can be formed with complete distinctiveness when they are joined together and written with great speed. The purpose of shorthand is to represent letters as briefly and as distinctively as possible. *The adoption of a uniform slope in a shorthand system would result in a confusing similarity of consonants,* and the hand of the writer would be retarded because of the necessity for careful and laborious representation of fine distinctions.

Shading of Consonants. In certain cases consonants are paired because of their similarity of sound. The first consonant in the pair is pronounced lightly (as "S"), and the second consonant in the pair is the corresponding heavy sound (as "Z"). The same stroke is used for both consonants, but for the first consonant a light stroke is written, and the second stroke of the pair is written with a slight pressure of the pen. *This use of shading avoids the necessity of employing different strokes to represent similarly sounded consonants.* If, for instance, half and double length strokes were used to represent these pairs, valuable shorthand abbreviating material would be lost, which in Pitman Shorthand is used to represent the addition of letters and even whole syllables. *The use of shading thus saves time and labor for the shorthand writer and shading in itself involves no extra penmanship.*

Elimination of Vowel Signs. Words are represented by a complete shorthand outline of their consonants. Contractions, or "wordsigns", are few in number. Circles, loops and hooks are used for the representation of frequently occurring and natural combinations of consonants in English words. In the application of this abbreviating material the presence or absence of a vowel is indicated, and it is unnecessary to write signs for the vowel sounds. *Here again the shorthand writer is saved much time and labor.* A series of disjoined vowel signs is provided for insertion where necessary, such as in isolated words, or proper names.

Position Writing. Position writing is a simple and effective device for the indication of vowels. Writing a word above, on, or through the line, according to its first vowel sound, *is another means of expressing sound without actual writing, and it is a device highly prized by the fastest writers.* Generations of the best writers in the world have proved that the most effective means of securing compact, swift, and legible shorthand outlines is through complete representation of the consonants, and that the insertion of the vowel signs is a needless waste of the writer's labor.

SUMMARY

In Pitman Shorthand the amount of actual writing has been reduced to a minimum because of the scientific use of the stenographic abbreviating material. Circles, loops, hooks, halving and doubling are devices used for the representation of syllables, and not for the formation of an alphabet. An adequate skill in shorthand writing is developed through the application of the abbreviating principles of the system. These devices are few in number, and they are easily understood and applied. Writers do not have to resort to such doubtful expedients as memorizing large numbers of specially contracted forms or writing only the first part of words, in order to keep pace with a speaker. They are able to develop their skill in accurate note taking without arbitrary memorization and with a minimum of labor. The simple principles of the system permit its writers to maintain and increase their skill, to their own satisfaction and to the satisfaction of those whose utterances they undertake to record.

Features of the Text

THIS TEXT presents the principles of Pitman Shorthand in a logical arrangement; the material provided for the use of students is arranged psychologically. The principles are stated briefly and simply, and each statement is followed by an adequate amount of application. The work of the teacher will be considerably facilitated by the division of the principles into small units of instruction.

An unusual feature of the text is the wealth of drill material provided for each unit of instruction. The amount of this material far exceeds that appearing in any shorthand text previously issued. The exercises have been so constructed that they are similar in context to the material that is dictated to the students in the later stages of the study of the subject. The development of skill in the reading and writing of these exercises is therefore of great importance, for they provide practice as valuable to the student as the dictation he will receive when the principles have been completed. Realization of this will encourage the student and will stimulate rapid progress. The exercises include a cumulative review of the principles and the short forms.

In the application of the principles a vocabulary of the two thousand commonest words has been used. Less frequently occurring words are used occasionally, however, to provide additional illustrations and to demonstrate, in the exercises, the application of a principle to similar words. These additional words are always well within the student's own vocabulary.

Most of the exercises are in shorthand, as it is felt that constant reading of correct shorthand forms is of the utmost value to the student. Experience indicates that it is advisable as far as possible to prevent students writing or seeing incorrectly written outlines, and for this reason the reading of correctly written shorthand, especially in the early stages, is of much importance. The shorthand plates are also useful for home assignments. Starting with Chapter Nine, longhand test material is included, and the teacher may find it advisable sometimes to dictate an exercise as new matter before it is read from the shorthand plate.

When the book has been completed, the *New Standard Dictation Course, Business Letters for Dictation,* or *The Expert Dictator,* will be found useful for the further development of skill in the writing of shorthand for business purposes. These dictation texts include word lists consisting of the third, fourth, and fifth thousand most frequently used words. Expert shorthand writers read as much printed shorthand literature as possible, in order to acquire an extensive shorthand vocabulary. A wide selection of such literature is available, and *Pitman's Journal*, issued monthly, includes many shorthand pages consisting of useful information for the shorthand writer.

The presentation of the principles and the exercise material in this text have been compiled and edited by John Bryant. The book is the result of close familiarity with the work of hundreds of teachers of wide experience, and the whole-hearted interest of these teachers, combined with their helpful observations and recommendations, have made this presentation possible.

CONTENTS

CHAPTER		PAGE
	INTRODUCTION	xii
I.	FIRST SIX CONSONANTS; $\bar{a}$ AND $\breve{e}$	1
II.	NEXT EIGHT CONSONANTS; $\bar{o}$ AND $\breve{u}$	4
III.	NEXT EIGHT CONSONANTS	6
IV.	FIRST-PLACE VOWELS	9
V.	THIRD-PLACE VOWELS	13
VI.	TWO FORMS FOR R	18
VII.	DIPHTHONGS AND H	25
VIII.	S CIRCLE	34
IX.	St AND Str LOOPS; Ses AND Sw CIRCLES; VOWEL INDICATION	44
X.	HALVING; DOWNWARD L; ABBREVIATED W	58
XI.	DOUBLE CONSONANTS	72
XII.	N AND F HOOKS	94
XIII.	*-Shun* HOOK	112
XIV.	COMPOUND CONSONANTS; TICK AND DOT H	122
XV.	HALVING AND DOUBLING	132
XVI.	PREFIXES AND SUFFIXES	145
XVII.	DIPHONES; MEDIAL W; SH, R, AND S	157
XVIII.	FIGURES; COMPOUND WORDS; INTERSECTIONS	164
	APPENDIX	171

Introduction

SHORTHAND is the art of representing spoken sounds by signs. Pitman Shorthand provides a sign for every sound heard in English words.

Ordinary longhand spelling is seldom phonetic. Pitman Shorthand is phonetic, that is, words are written exactly as they are sounded, and not according to the ordinary longhand spelling. No letters are used that are not wanted to represent the sound. The following illustrations show how to spell when writing shorthand—

palm is spelled *pahm* *wrought* is spelled *rawt*

pale " " *pāl* *coal* " " *kōl*

key " " *kē* *tomb* " " *toom*

The shorthand characters should be made as neatly and as accurately as possible. The size of the shorthand strokes in this text is a good standard to adopt in your own writing. The signs join readily with one another, and they can be written with great speed when you have practiced them sufficiently. Resist the temptation to sacrifice neatness for speed. Speed in writing will naturally follow the practice of neat and accurate writing.

CHAPTER I
Pitman Shorthand Alphabet

1. The First Six Consonants

The sounds heard in English words are divided as follows:

>Twenty-four Consonants
>Twelve Vowels
>Four Diphthongs

A shorthand sign is provided for each of these sounds.

The first six consonants are represented by straight strokes written downward:

Letter	Sign	Name	As in
P		pee	pay, ape, up
B		bee	bay, Abe, be
T		tee	Tay, ate, it
D		dee	day, aid, do
CH		chay	chest, etch, which
J		jay	jest, edge, age

The arrows indicate the direction in which the strokes are written. **They are never** written in any other direction.

>NOTE. These consonants form pairs: *p* and *b*, *t* and *d*, *ch* and *j*. In each pair a *light* sound is represented by a *light* stroke, and a corresponding *heavy* sound is represented by a *heavier* stroke.

2. Vowel ā

Vowels are represented by dots and dashes written alongside the consonant strokes. When a vowel comes *before* a consonant, it is placed *before* the stroke (left side); when a vowel comes *after* a consonant, it is placed *after* the stroke (right side).

The long vowel *ā* is represented by a heavy dot:

\ ape \ pay \ Abe \ bay | ate | aid | day / age

Write the consonant stroke first, and then place the vowel sign. Two light dashes underneath an outline indicate a proper name.

> NOTE: There are three places alongside a stroke in which vowels may be written—beginning, middle, and end, or, first, second, and third place. The dot for long *ā* is written in the middle place, and it is therefore called a "second-place vowel."

3. Joining of Consonants

Consonants are joined without lifting the pen, as in longhand. Begin the second where the first ends, and write the stroke in its proper direction. Note that the first stroke rests on the line.

> p ch   bt   tp   dt   ch p   bd   dp   jt
> paid   page   bait   babe   tape   date

4. Vowel ĕ

Short *ĕ* is represented by a light dot, and is a second-place vowel:

etch   edge   bet   pep   Ted   debt   jet

Note that the first stroke rests on the line. Write the consonant outline first, and then place the vowel sign.

5. Short Forms for Common Words

A few very frequently used words, such as *be, it, the, to,* are expressed in shorthand by a single sign. These short forms promote speedy writing, and they should be thoroughly memorized.

\ be | it | do   / which   . the   \ to   \ two or too

| but   / who

6. Phrasing

As an aid to rapid writing, shorthand words may often be joined. This is called phrasing. Outlines should be phrased only when they join easily and naturally, as shown in the examples throughout this textbook. The first word in a phrase is written in its normal position:

to do   but which

A small tick *at the end* of a word represents *the*. The tick is written either upward or downward, whichever forms the sharper angle:

to the   be the   do the   which the   pay the   paid the

7. Punctuation

The following special punctuation marks are used in shorthand:

×	؟	!	=	⌒	( )
period	question	exclamation	hyphen	dash	parenthesis

Other signs are written as in longhand.

EXERCISE 1

CHAPTER II

8. The Second Group of Consonants

The next four pairs of consonants are curves, and they are written downward:

Letter	Sign	Name	As in	Short Form for
F		ef	few, safe, for	
V		vee	view, save, have	have
TH		ith	thigh, bath, think	think
TH		thee	thy, bathe, them	them
S		ess	seal, ice, us	
Z		zee	zeal, eyes, was	was
SH		ish	she, wish, shall	shall
ZH		zhee	measure, treasure, usual	usual or usually

(a) they, say, fade, faith, shape, bathe, shade

(b) fed, fetch, death, shed, essay

9. Vowels ō and ŭ

Long ō is represented by a heavy dash, and is a second-place vowel:

toe, oat, bow, Joe, foe, oath, so, owes, show, showed, boat, both, vote

Short ŭ is represented by a light dash, and is a second-place vowel:

up, us, tub, touch, Dutch, judge

EXERCISE 2

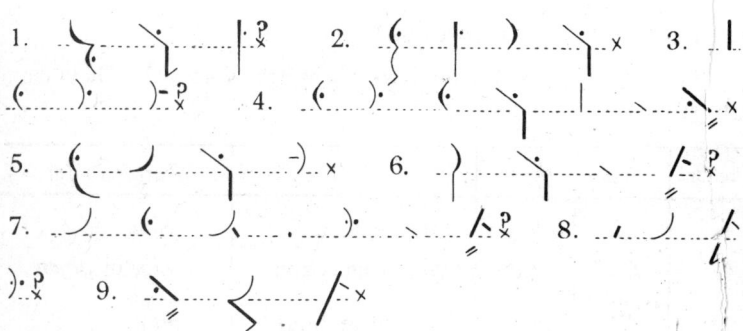

EXERCISE 3

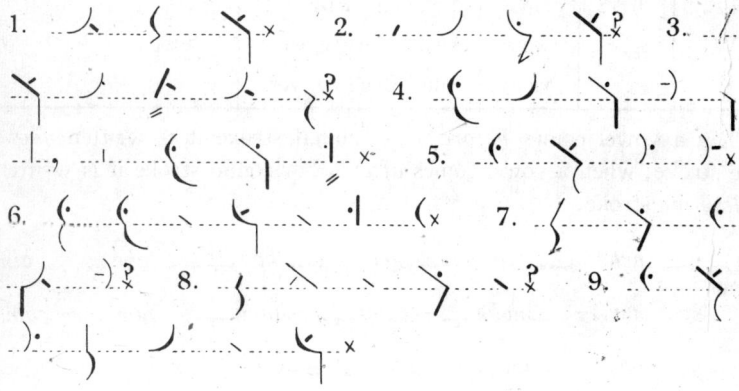

CHAPTER III

10. The Next Eight Consonants

The next eight consonants are all written forward. They are all light strokes except *g* and *ng*:

Letter	Sign	Name	As in	Short Form for
K		kay	cane, leak, come	come
G		gay	gain, league, give	give or given
M		em	may, seem, him	him
N		en	nay, seen, no	
NG		ing	long, sing, thing	thing
L		el	lay, coal, will	
W		way	weigh, aware, we	we
Y		yay	youth, yellow, yes	

When a vowel comes *before* a horizontal stroke it is written *above* the stroke; when a vowel comes *after* a horizontal stroke it is written *below* the stroke.

(a) ache, egg, gay, keg, cake, aim, may, make, came, game, gum, comb, no, know, name, neck

(b) ail, lay, laid, led, lake, delay, low, load, below, love, luck, lung, coal, goal, mail

(c) way, weigh, woe, web, wed, wedge, yoke, yellow

(d) take check joke became beg

shake folk shame thumb lunch

bunch change length tongue

In a phrase, the stroke *l* is used to represent the word *will*:

it will which will who will they will

it will be it will have they will be

they will have, etc.

EXERCISE 4

1. ... 2. ...
3. ... 4. ...
5. ...
6. ... 7. ...

EXERCISE 5

1. ... 2. ...
3. ...
4. ...

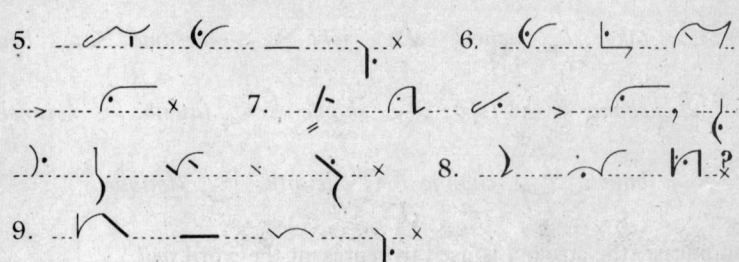

EXERCISE 6

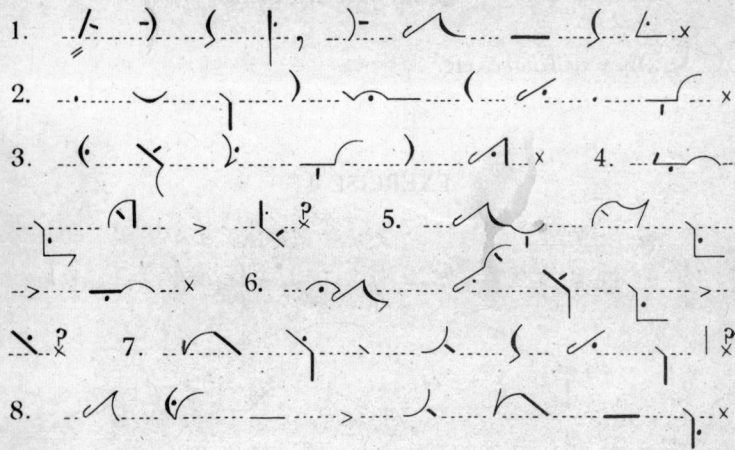

CHAPTER IV

11. First-Place Vowels

The next four vowels are written in the *first* place, that is, at the beginning of a stroke. When the *first* vowel in a word is a *first-place* vowel, the outline is written in *first* position, that is, the first downstroke or upstroke in the outline is written *above* the line. First position outlines consisting of horizontal strokes are written above the line.

(*a*) Long *ah* is represented by a heavy dot:

　pa　　*ma*　　*calm*　　*palm*

(*b*) Short *ă* is represented by a light dot:

　at　*add*　*path*　*pal*　*pack*　*back*　*bath*
　attack　*attach*　*tank*　*bank*　*damage*　*shadow*
　catch　*cash*　*gang*　*am*　*among*　*map*
　away　*lack*　*manage*　*annum*　*package*

(*c*) Long *aw* is represented by a heavy dash:

　saw　*paw*　*ball*　*bought*　*talk*　*tall*
　auto　*chalk*　*jaw*　*law*

(*d*) Short *ŏ* is represented by a light dash:

　top　*odd*　*doll*　*dog*　*job*　*off*　*shock*
　shop　*got*　*lodge*　*lock*　*long*　*knock*
　watch　*wash*

SHORT FORMS

_for *a* or *an* of on had or dollar on the but the (the signs for *on* and *but* slightly slanted)

EXERCISE 7

EXERCISE 8

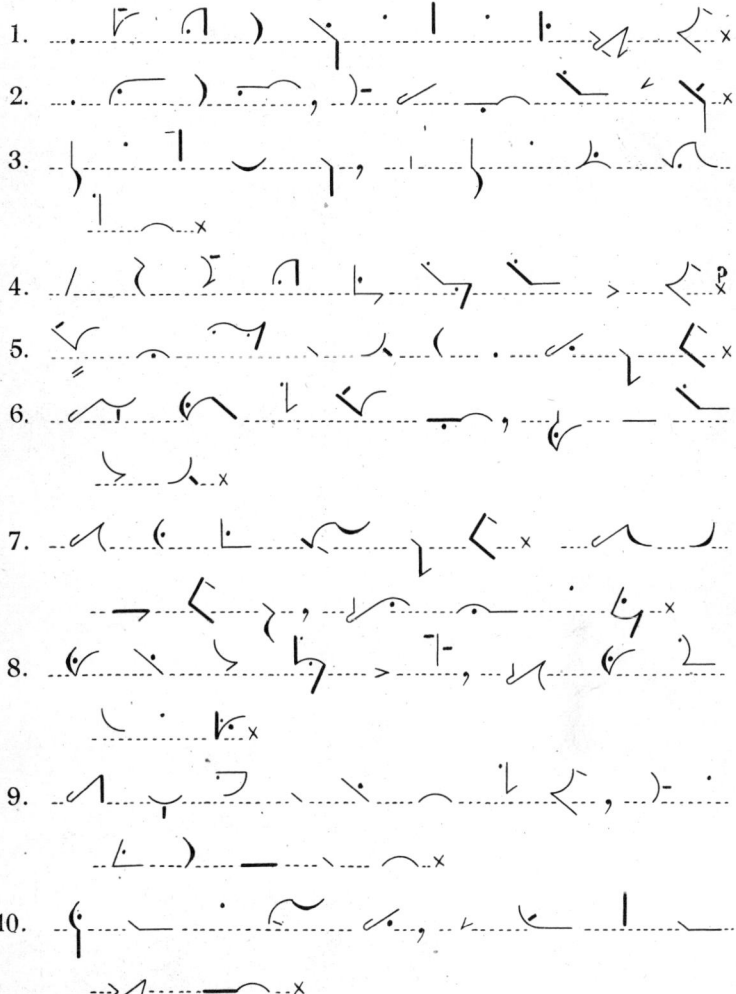

12. Second Position

When a *second-place* vowel is the *first* vowel in a word, the outline is written in *second* position, that is, the first downstroke or upstroke rests on the line:

get — *enough* — *Monday* — *engage* — *month* — *envelope* — *cup* — *leg* — *detail* — *coal* — *take*

EXERCISE 9

1.
2.
3.
4.
5.
6.
7.
8.
9.
10.

PITMAN SHORTHAND

CHAPTER V

13. Third-Place Vowels

The last four vowels are written in the third place. When a third-place vowel comes between two strokes, it is put in third place before the second stroke.

When a third-place vowel is the first vowel in a word, the outline is written in third position, that is, the first downstroke or upstroke is written through the line.

(a) Long ē is represented by a heavy dot:

eat   tea   each   see   she   ease   fee
feed   deep   keep   leave   teach   theme
deal   meal   team

(b) Short ĭ is represented by a light dot:

if   bit   pick   big   ship   live   inch
kid   ill   bill   mill   milk   thick   width

(c) Long ōō is represented by a heavy dash:

chew   shoe   food   move   youth   tool
pool   cool   tooth

(d) Short ŏŏ is represented by a light dash:

book   took   look   wood   pull   push

baby   lucky   money   copy   many   lady
family   fifty   monthly   daily   appeal

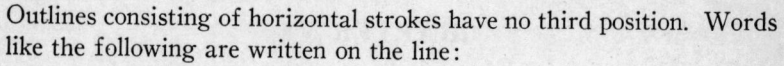

Outlines consisting of horizontal strokes have no third position. Words like the following are written on the line:

___. key___ .kick ___ cook ___ ink ___ King

Drop the ĭ vowel in the termination *-ing*:

___ making ___ taking ___ leaving ___ living ___ looking
___ asking ___ mailing ___ talking ___ washing

SHORT FORMS

___ *different* or *difference* ___ *wish* ___ *put* ___ *to be* ___ *owe*
___ *can* ___ *go* ___ *ought* ___ *in* or *any*

Short Form Derivatives: ___ *being* ___ *doing* ___ *having* ___ *going*

EXERCISE 10

PITMAN SHORTHAND

7.

8.

9.

10.

11.

12.

EXERCISE 11

1.

2.

3.

4.

5.

6.

7. 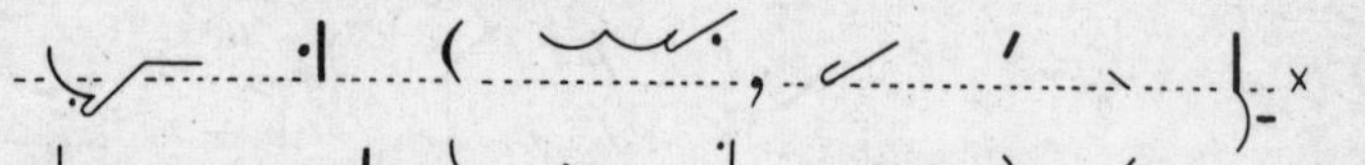

8. 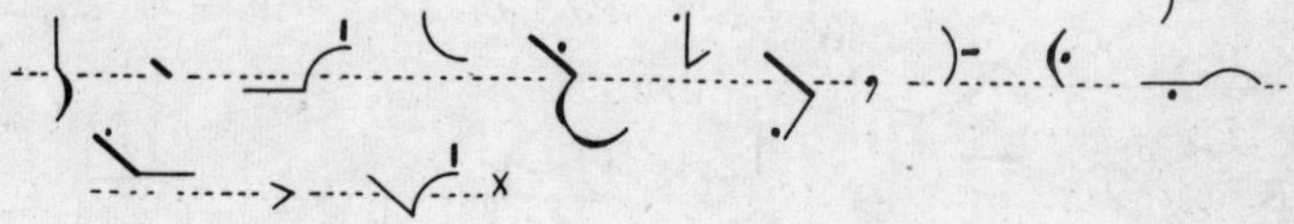

9. 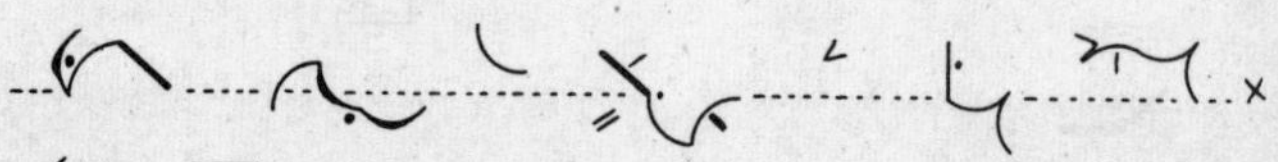

10. 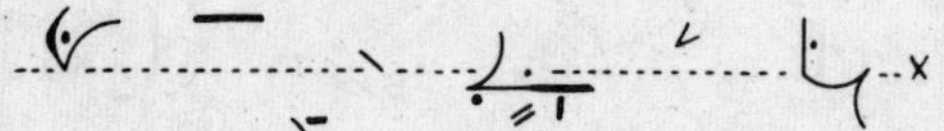

11. 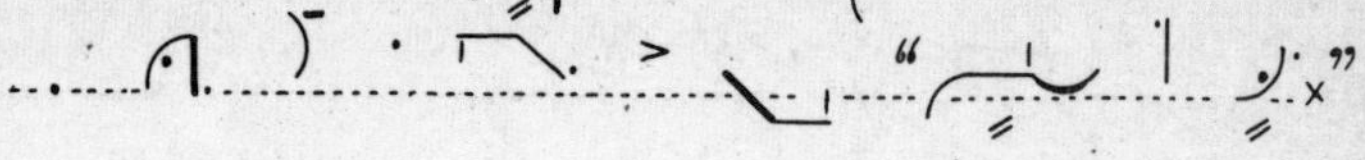

12. 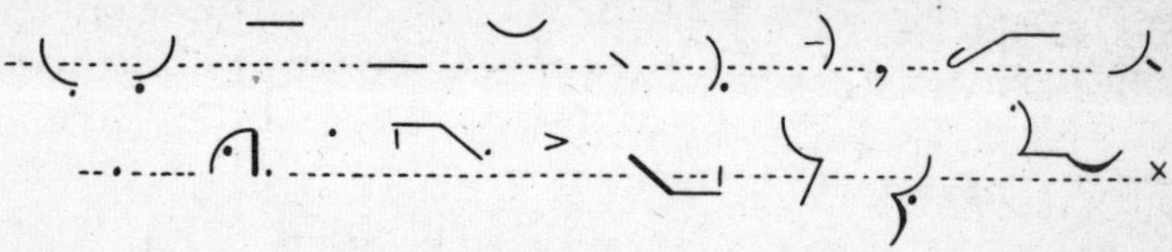

EXERCISE 12

1. 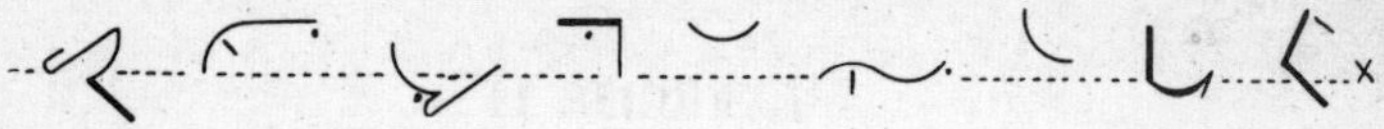

2. 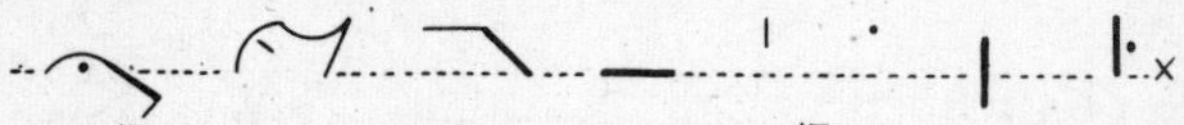

3. 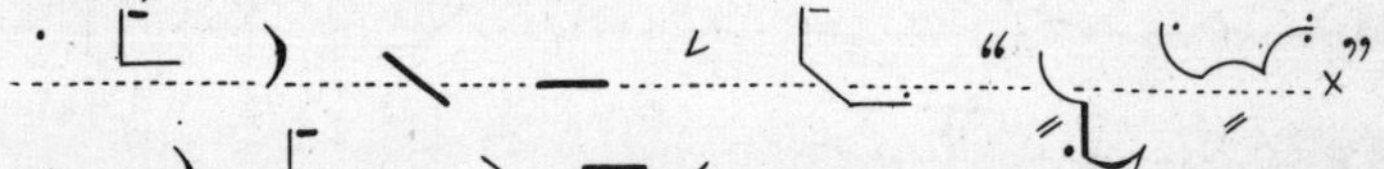

4. 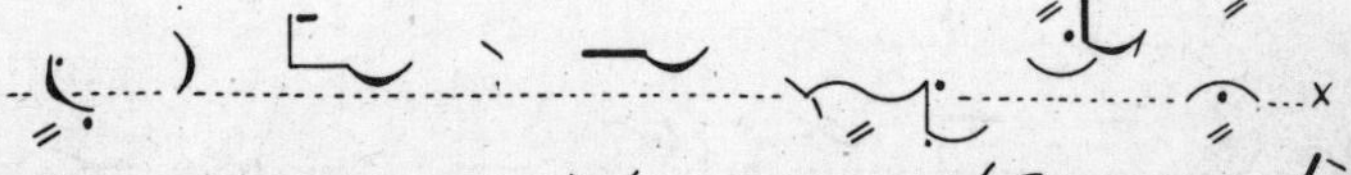

5. 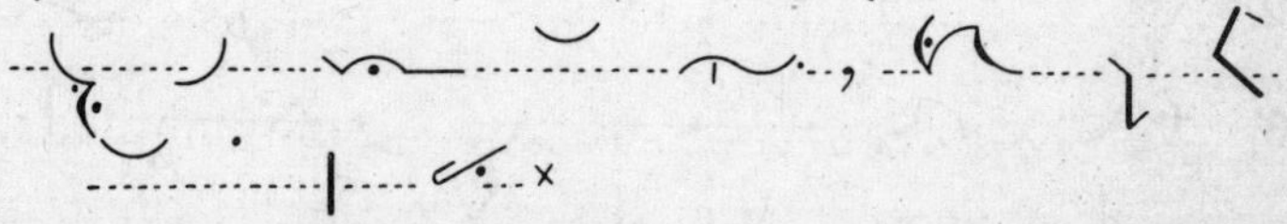

6. 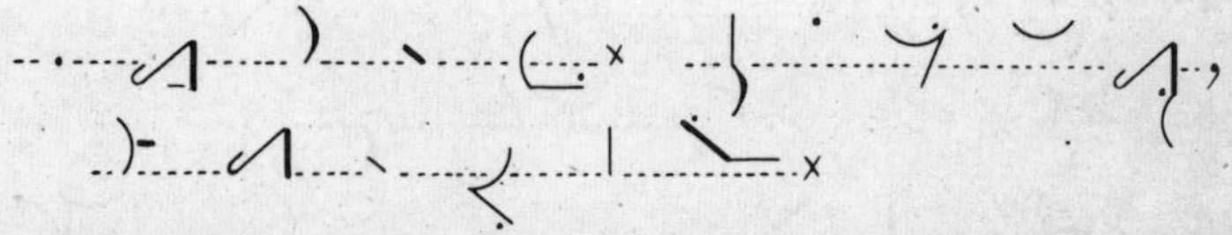

7. 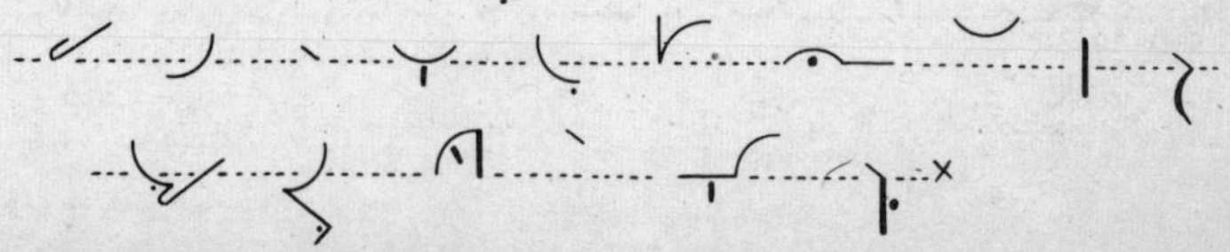

PITMAN SHORTHAND

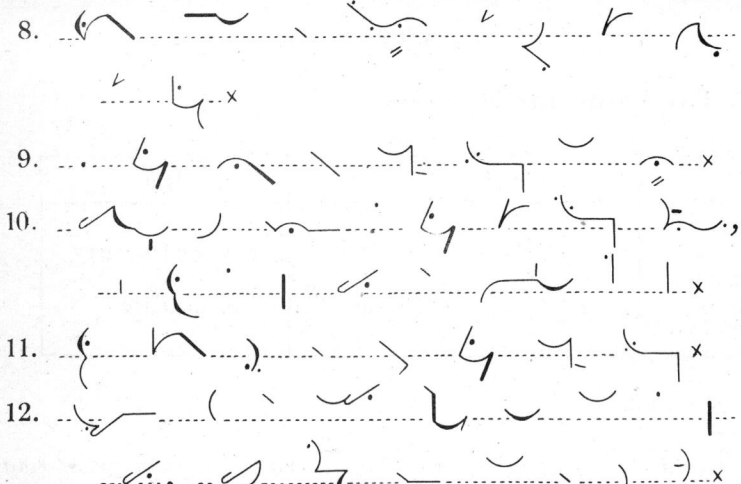

CHAPTER VI

14. Two Forms for R

Letter	Sign	Name	As in
R	⤴	ray	raw, reach, carry
	⤵	ar	car, air, dare

When *r* begins a word use ⟋:

⟋ red ⟋ raw ⟋ road ⟋ rug ⟋ rush ⟋ ring

⟋ reach ⟋ ready ⟋ readily ⟋ retail ⟋ wrong

⟋ railroad ⟋ range ⟋ rank ⟋ relief ⟋ relieve

⟋ rich ⟋ reading

When a word begins with the combination *"vowel-r"* use ⤵ :

⤵ air ⤵ arm ⤵ or ⤵ ear ⤵ early ⤵ army

SHORT FORMS

⟋ (up) *are* ⟋ (up) *our* or *hour* ⟋ (up) *and* ⟋ (up) *should*

NOTE: *Chay* and *Ray:* These strokes are somewhat similar, but they are different in slope and in the direction in which they are written. *Chay* is always written downward at a small angle from the vertical.

Ray is always written upward at a small angle from the horizontal.

PITMAN SHORTHAND

EXERCISE 13

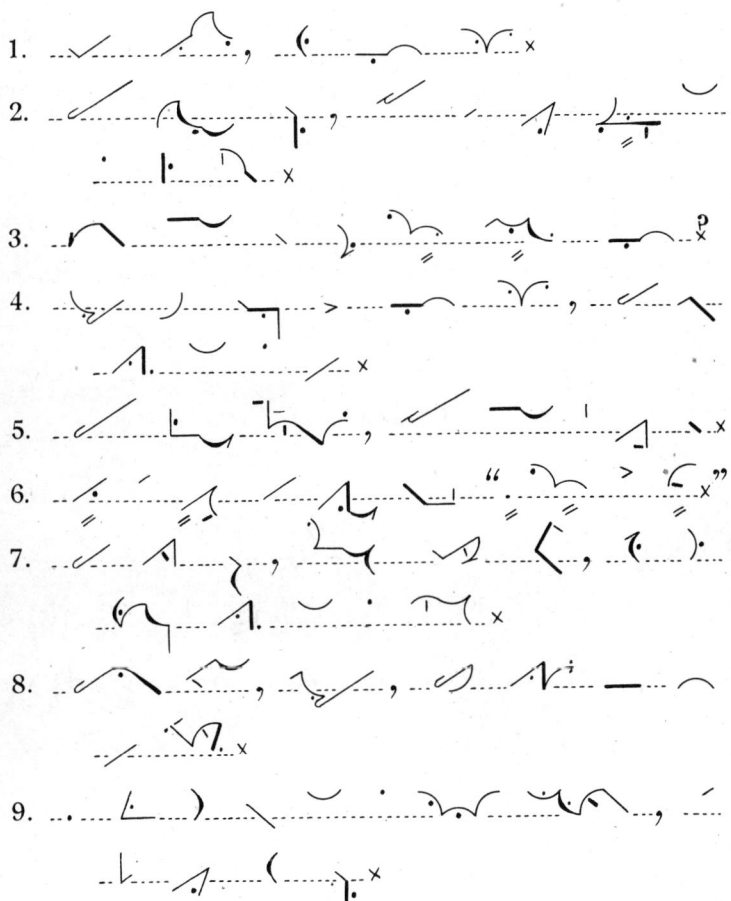

15. When *r* ends a word use ⌒ :

car, far, pair, share, dare, per, error, bear, chair, door, affair, appear, fare, fear, four, fur, repair, assure

When a word ends with the combination *"r-vowel"* use ..⟋..:

.⁀.. *carry* ⁀.. *marry* ⌵.. *ferry* ⌒⁀.. *memory* ⌒⌵.. *factory*
⌵.. *injury* .⁀.. *borrow* ⌵.. *dairy* ⌵.. *jury* ⁀⌵.. *narrow*
⌵.. *thorough* ⌵.. *vary* ⌒⌵.. *tomorrow*

SHORT FORMS

⌒).. *your* ⌒).. *year* .).. *whose* ⁄.. *large* (.. *thank* or *thanked*

NOTE: In the phrase *"to go"* .⌐.. the vowel is inserted.

EXERCISE 14

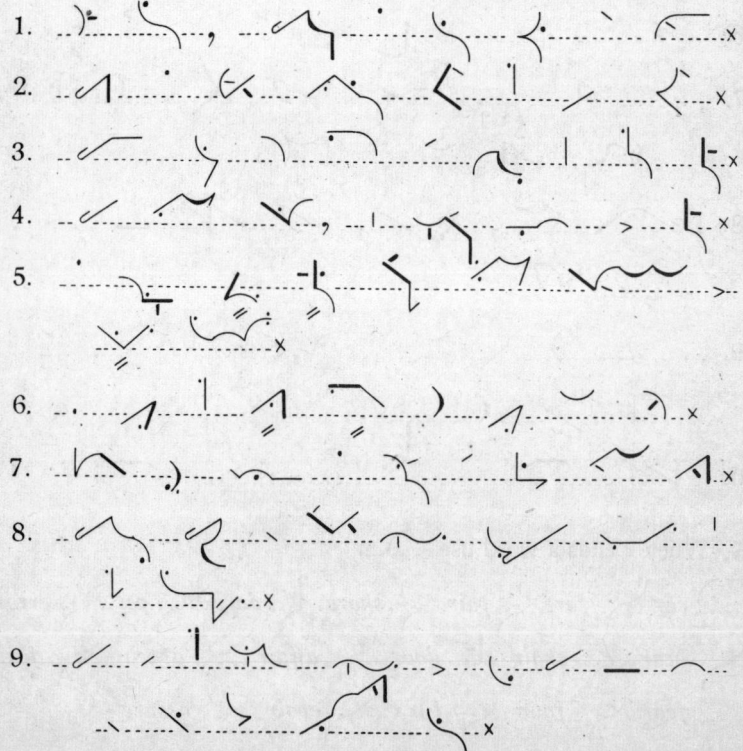

PITMAN SHORTHAND

10. [shorthand outlines]
11. [shorthand outlines]
12. [shorthand outlines]
13. [shorthand outlines]
14. [shorthand outlines]
15. [shorthand outlines]

16. In order to avoid awkward joinings *r* is written

(*a*) Downward before *m:*

[shorthand] *room* [shorthand] *Rome* [shorthand] *remedy* [shorthand] *form* [shorthand] *firm* [shorthand] *alarm* [shorthand] *remove*

(*b*) Upward before *ch, j* and *th:*

[shorthand] *arch* [shorthand] *urge* [shorthand] *earth*

(*c*) Upward after a straight upstroke:

[shorthand] *rear* [shorthand] *rare* [shorthand] *roar* [shorthand] *aware* [shorthand] *career* [shorthand] *lawyer*

(*d*) Usually it is better to write upward *r* in the middle of a word:

[shorthand] *March* [shorthand] *party* [shorthand] *forty* [shorthand] *authority* [shorthand] *charge* [shorthand] *garage* [shorthand] *fourth* [shorthand] *mark* [shorthand] *parade* [shorthand] *thoroughly*

EXERCISE 15

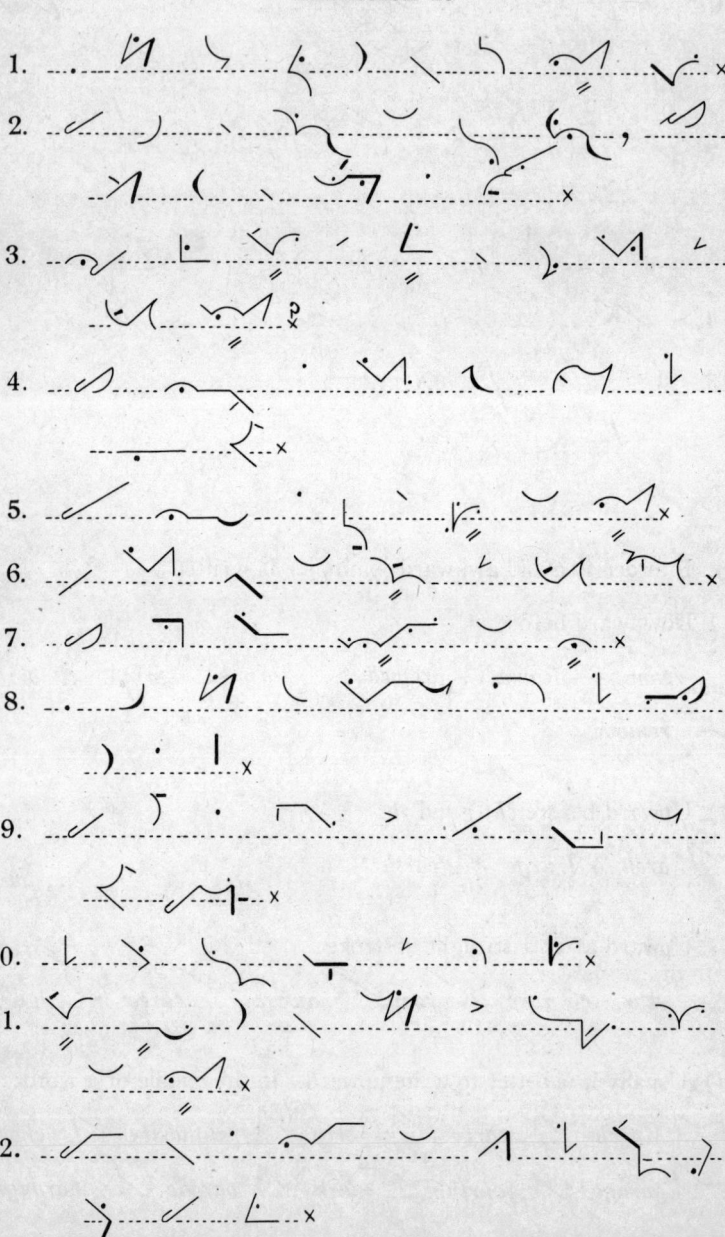

PITMAN SHORTHAND

EXERCISE 16

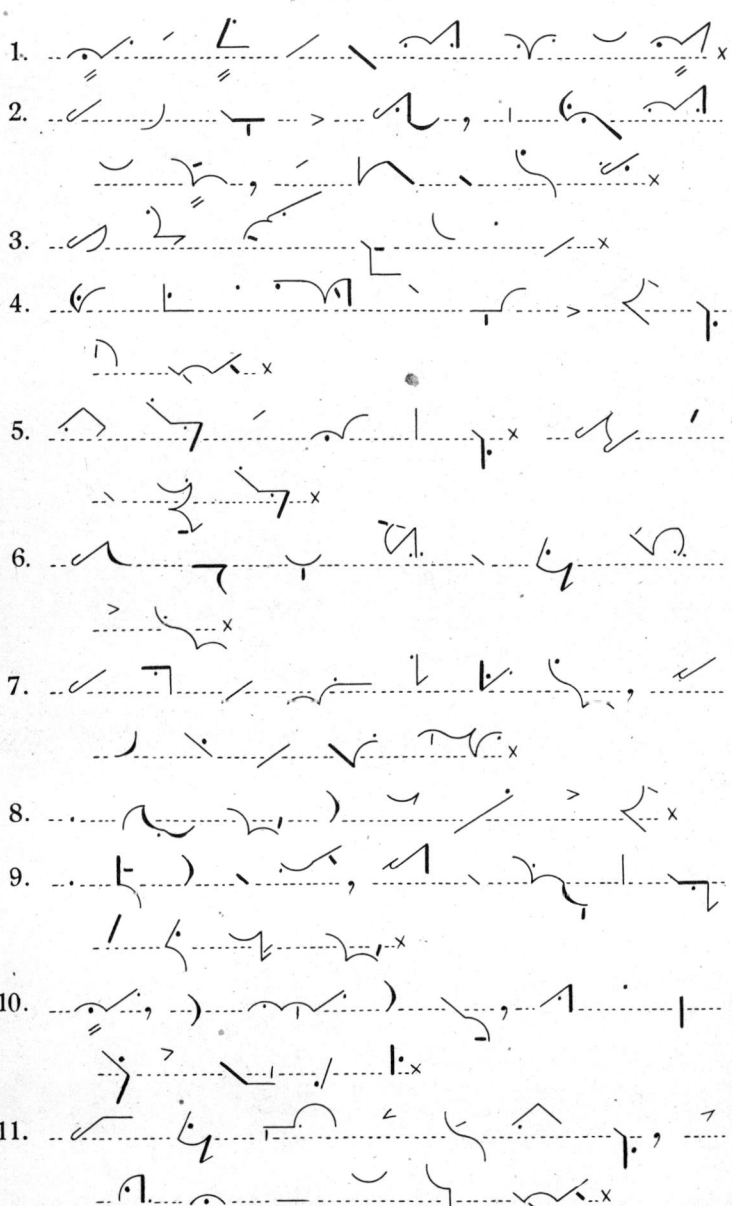

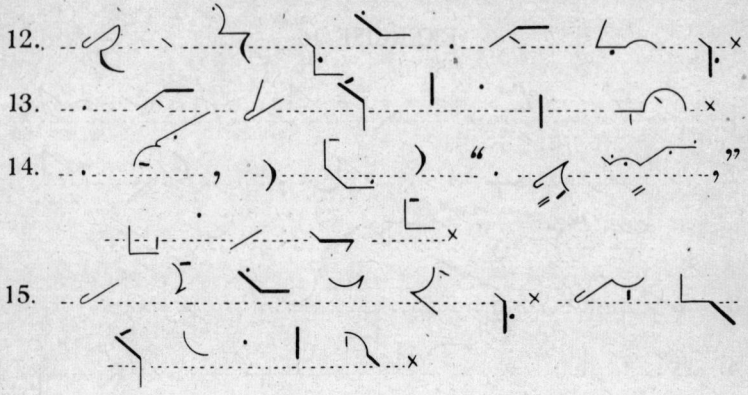

CHAPTER VII

17. Diphthongs

The four diphthongs (or double vowels) are *i, oi, ow,* and *u,* as heard in the words *I enjoy Gow's music.*

(*a*) The diphthong *i* is represented by a small angular mark written in the first vowel place:

pie, pipe, tie, type, die, by, buy, time, my, wide, lie, like, admire, alive, fire, five, tire, retire, arrive, pile, bite, dime, rye, knife, mile, china, shy, ripe

(*b*) The diphthong *oi* is represented by the same sign turned on its side. It is also written in the first vowel place:

boy, joy, enjoy, toy, boil, boiler, annoy, coil, toil, coy, alloy

(*c*) The diphthong *ow* is written as shown, in the third vowel place:

cow, out, loud, mouth, row, couch, outlay, lounge, county

(*d*) The diphthong *u* is represented by a small semicircle written in the third vowel place:

beauty, duty, failure, cure, endure, cube, bureau, tube, occupy

SHORT FORMS

I, eye,   how   why   beyond   you   with   when   what   would   me

EXERCISE 17

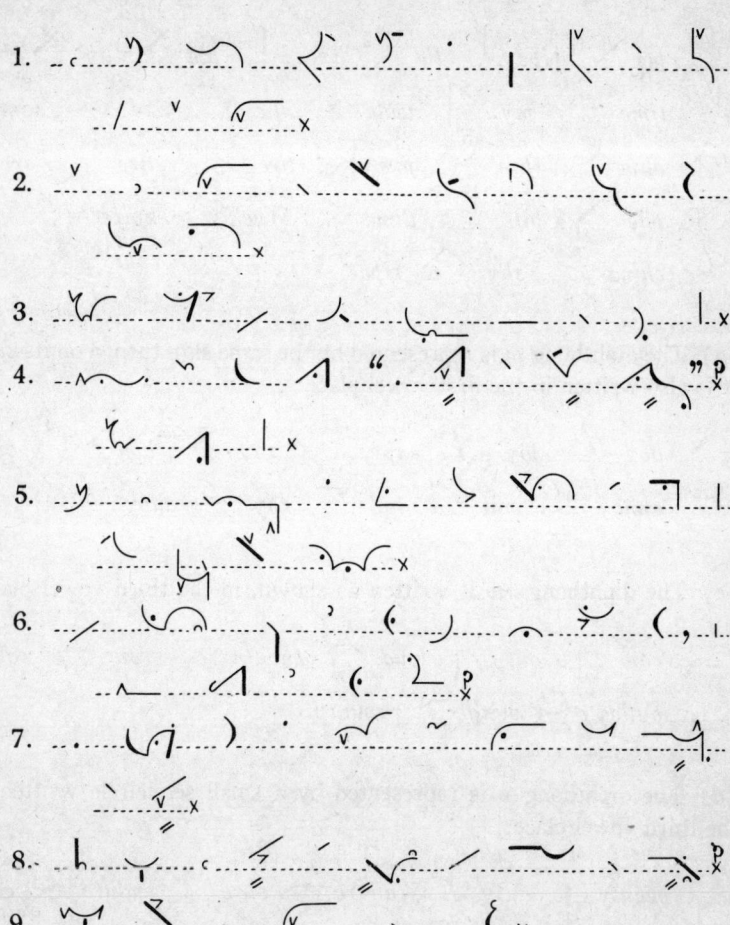

PITMAN SHORTHAND

10.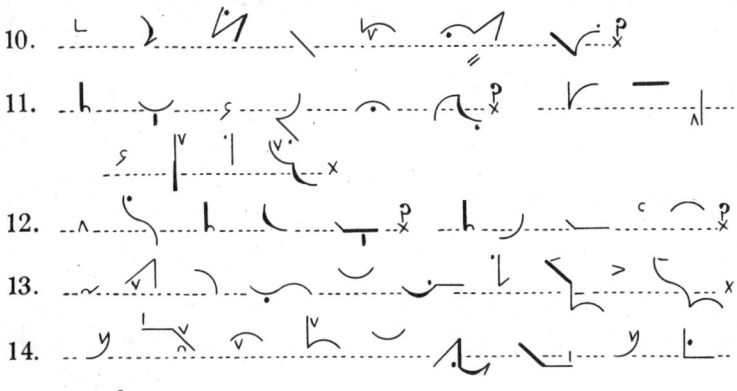
11.
12.
13.
14.

EXERCISE 18

1. 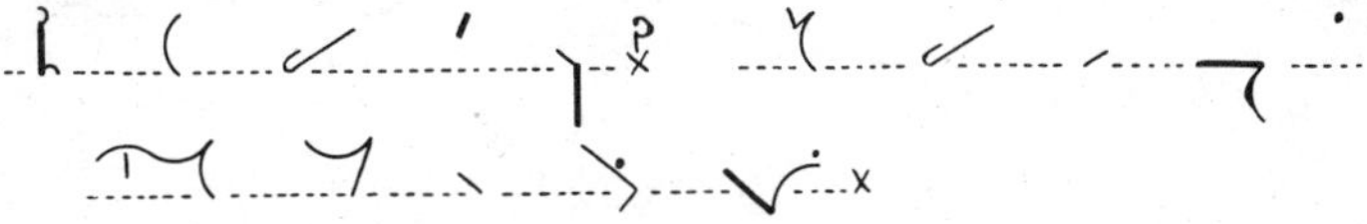
2. 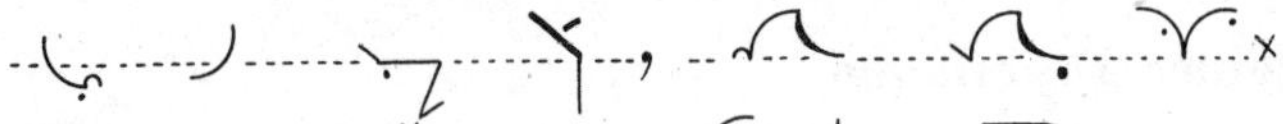
3. 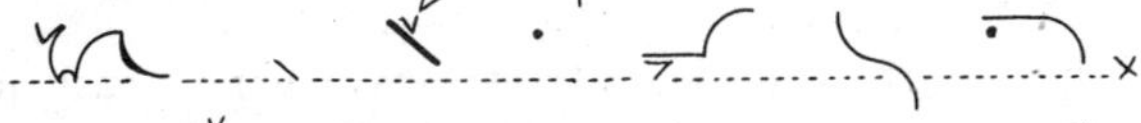
4. 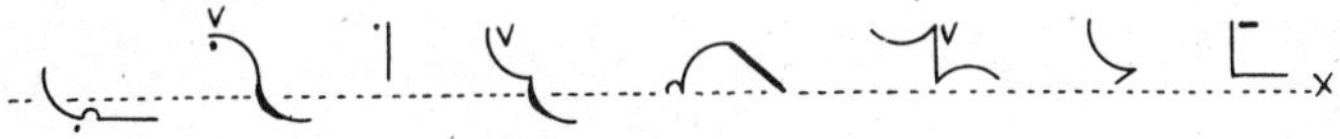
5. 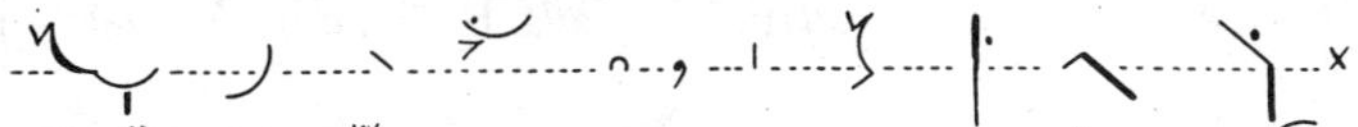
6. 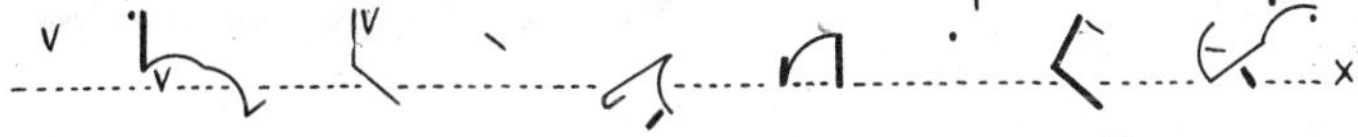
7. 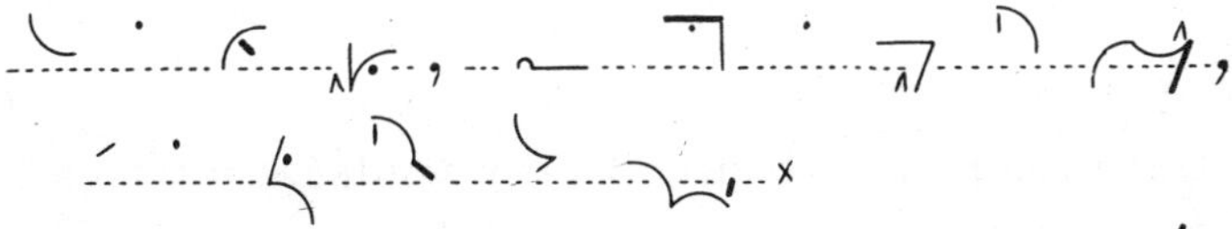
8. 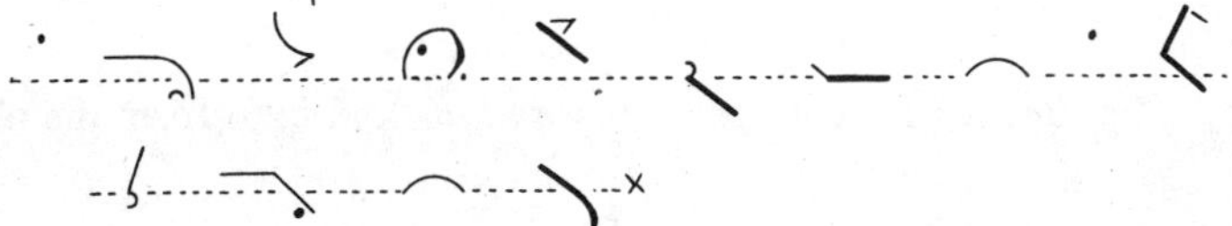
9.

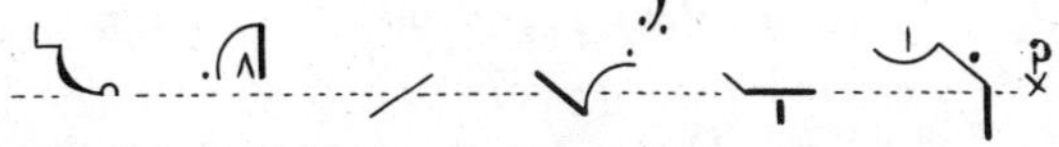

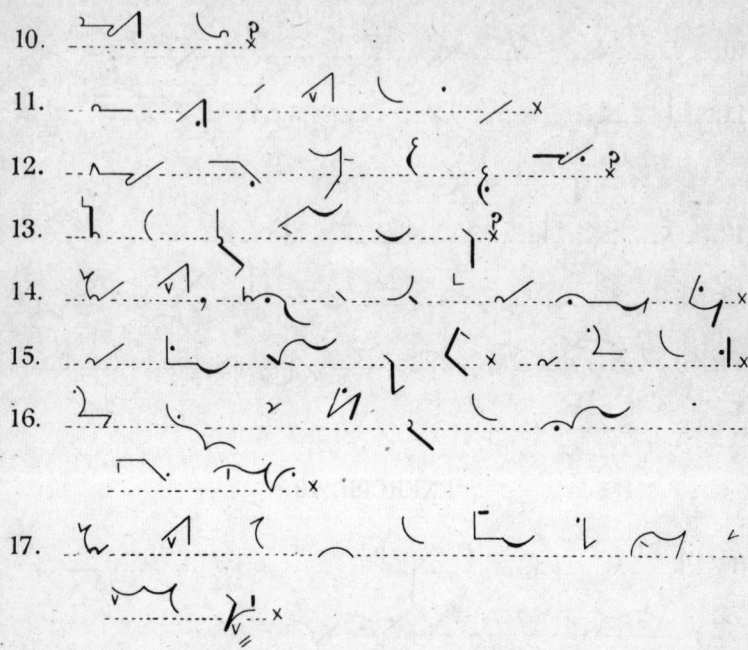

18. Joined Diphthongs

(a) The diphthong signs are joined to strokes when an easy joining can be made:

ice   eyes   item   idle   deny   oil   due   few   issue   new   avenue   review   value   renew   revenue   bough or bow.

(b) The sign for *ow* is contracted in the word now.

(c) The sign for *i* is contracted before *l*, *m*, and *k*, to form the phrases

 I will (I'll)   *I am (I'm)*   *I may*   *I can*

PITMAN SHORTHAND

(d) The short form *you* is turned on its side to form the phrases

can you *give you* *with you* *when you* *what you* *would you* *are you*

19. Triphones

A small tick added to a diphthong sign indicates another vowel following the diphthong:

buying *dying* *lying* *via* *Iowa* *loyal* *voyage* *enjoying* *power* *shower* *tower* *towel* *fewer* *issuing*

EXERCISE 19

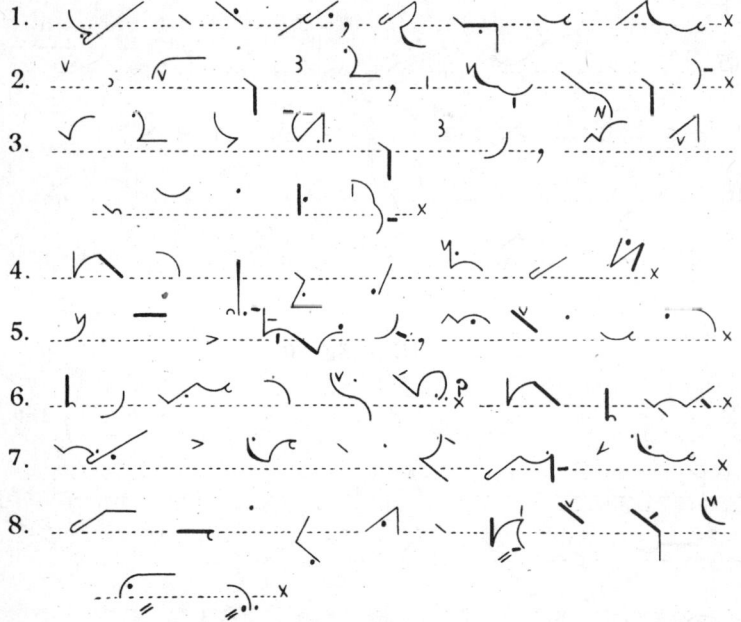

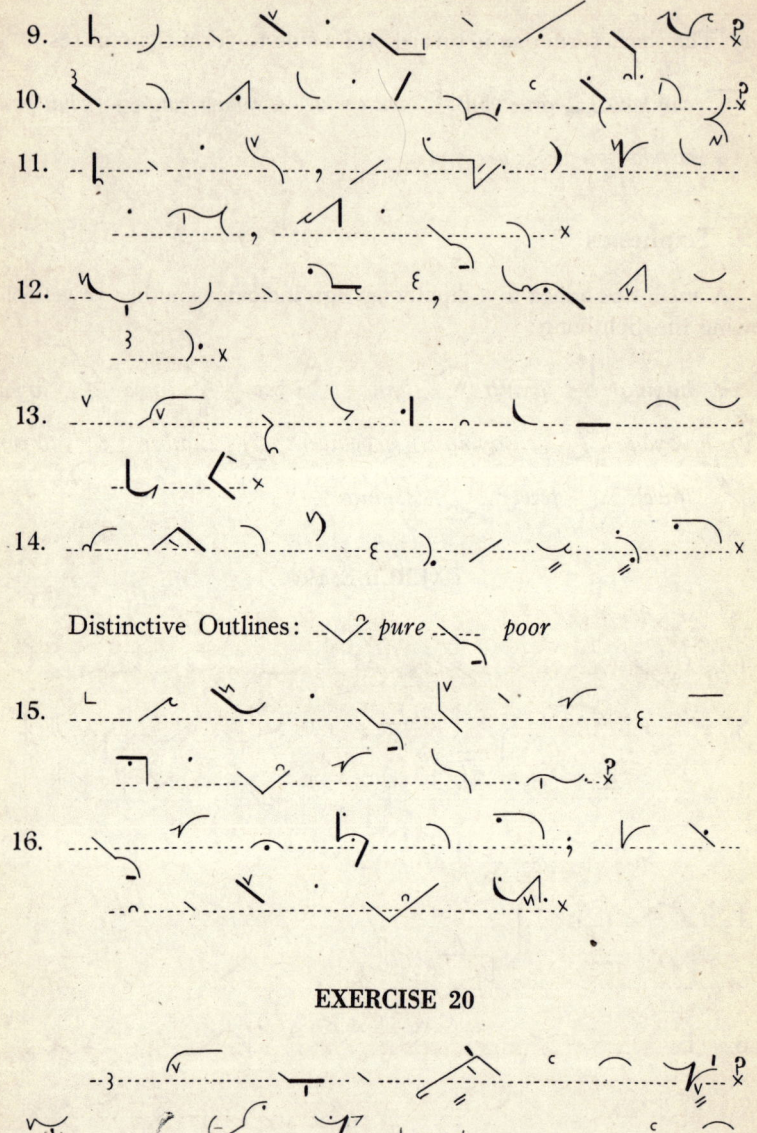

Distinctive Outlines: pure   poor

EXERCISE 20

PITMAN SHORTHAND

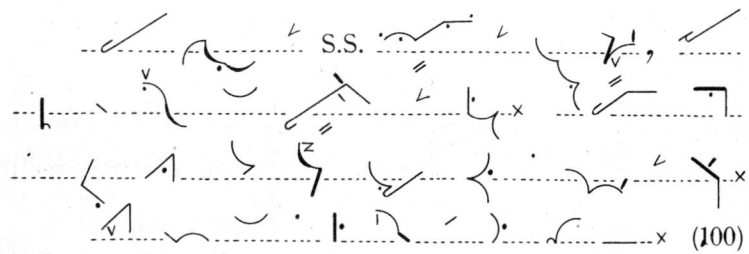

(100)

EXERCISE 21

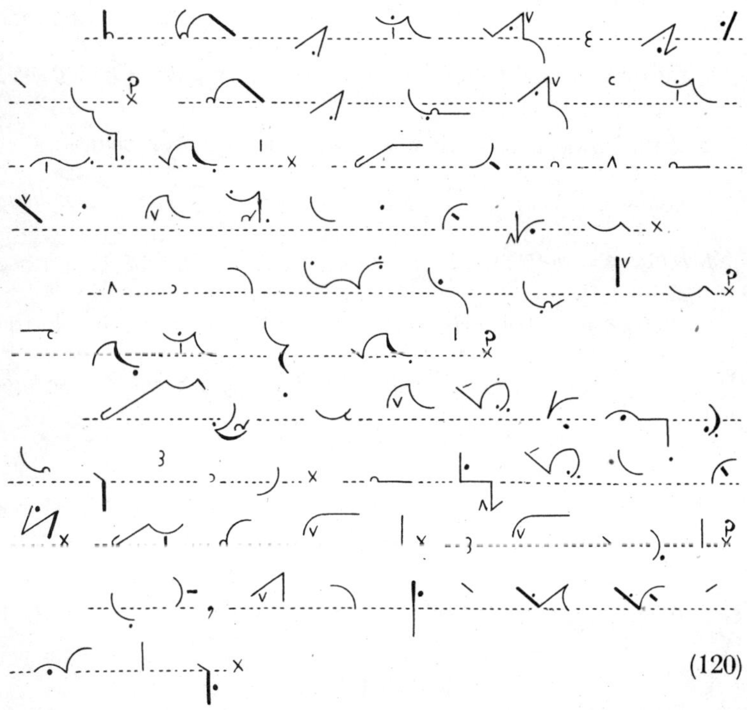

(120)

20. Consonant H

Letter	Sign	Name	As in
H		hay	he, high, hay
		hay	hope, happy, head

(a) When *h* is the only consonant stroke, or is followed by *k* or *g*, use the downward form:

he, hay, Ohio, high, hake, Haig, and the derivatives of *high*: highly, higher, highway

(b) Use the upward form when *h* is joined to other consonants:

happy, hope, head, heavy, hotel, hang, huge, hurry

(c) The word *hope* is contracted to the stroke *p* to form the phrases

I hope, I hope you will, I hope you are, we hope, we hope you will, we hope you are, etc.

(d) The word *he* is represented in the middle or at the end of a phrase by the short form . In other cases is used.

if he, if he should, but he will

EXERCISE 22

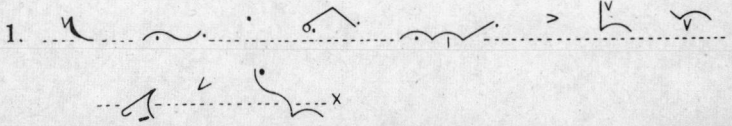

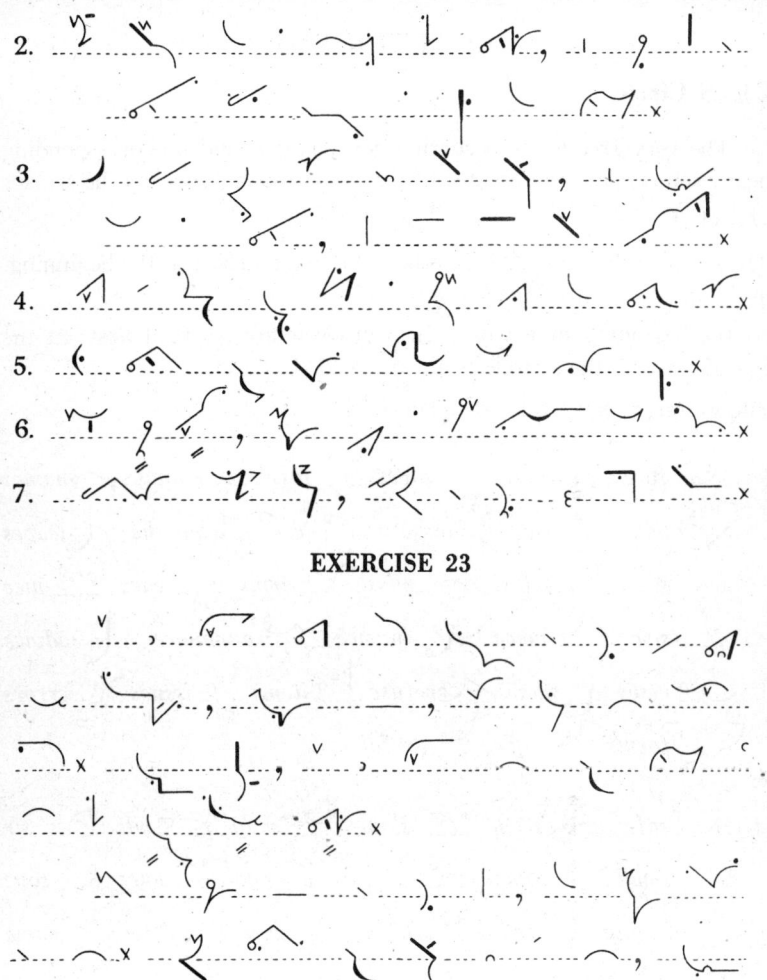

EXERCISE 23

(82)

CHAPTER VIII

21. S Circle

The very frequently occurring consonant *s*, and its corresponding heavy sound *z*, are represented by a small circle as well as by the strokes ..)..and ..)..

The small circle joins easily to other consonant strokes at the beginning, in the middle, or at the end of a word.

At the beginning of a word, the *s* circle is always read first; at the end of a word, the *s* circle is always read last.

The *s* circle is written inside a curve:

(a) face these shoes loss knows names bills else anxious less months leaves shows lose miss arms ears nice size voice invoice announce advice news views refuse items issues errors forms office affairs

(b) safe seem slow song silk sir small Sunday sense sale sales save saving sell selling sleep snow some soon sun since similar soil south sign salary

(c) message absence business cousin reason receive receiving passing dozen inside music Wednesday

SHORT FORMS

has, or as   his, or is   several   those   this   thus

NOTE: has the, or as the   is the

EXERCISE 24

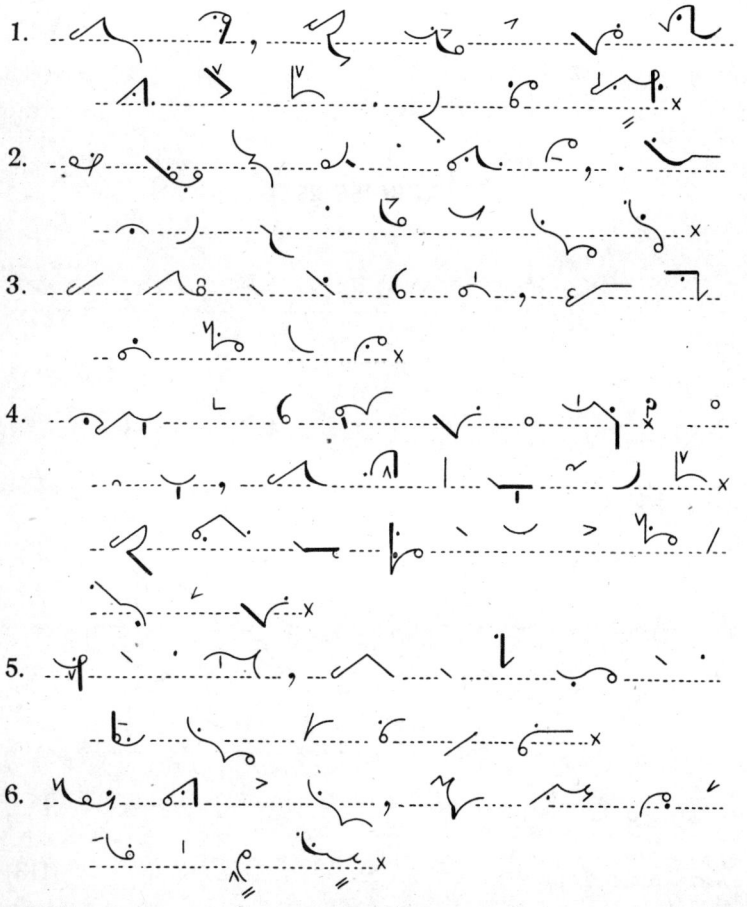

EXERCISE 25

22. The *s* circle is written with a left motion to straight strokes.

(*a*) This means that it is written on the right side of straight downstrokes:

pass, *days*, *copies*, *ladies*, *inches*, *piece*, *pages*, *choose*, *sat*, *said*, *sets*, *speech*, *such*, *sad*, *sit*, *city*, *cities*, *stay*, *spare*, *Saturday*, *side*, *suit*, *etc.* (et cetera), *outside*, *decide*, *Tuesday*

(*b*) It is written on the upper side of straight horizontal strokes and straight upstrokes:

guess, *looks*, *box*, *fix*, *folks*, *case*, *cause*, *sick*, *soak*, *six*, *sake*, *secure*, *schedule*, *excuse*, *use*, *ways*, *yes*, *raise*, *house*, *carries*, *marries*, *varies*, *twice*, *sorry*, *series*, *service*

SHORT FORMS

because, *special*, or *specially*, *speak*, *subject*, or *subjected*

The *s* circle is added to short forms:

speaks, *subjects*, *yours*, *years*, *ours*, or *hours*, *wishes*, *thinks*, *thanks*, *goes*, *gives*, *comes*, *dollars*, *things*, *differences*, *puts*, etc.

EXERCISE 26

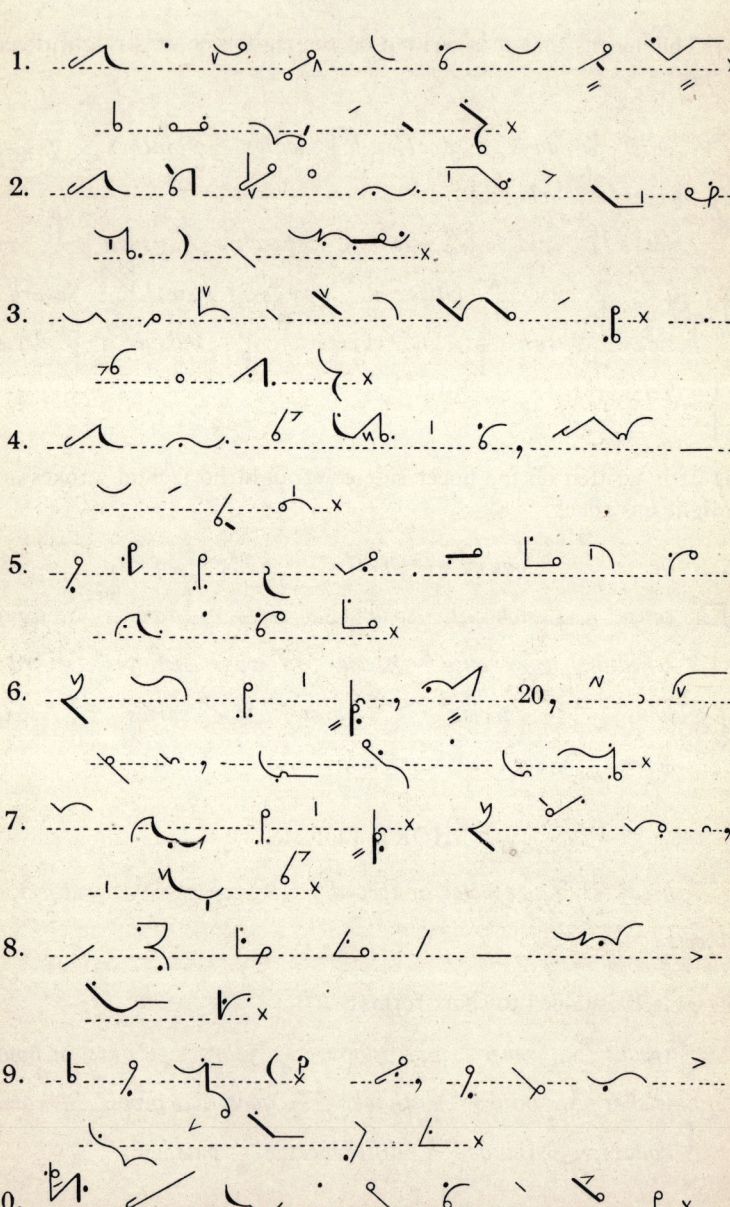

PITMAN SHORTHAND

EXERCISE 27

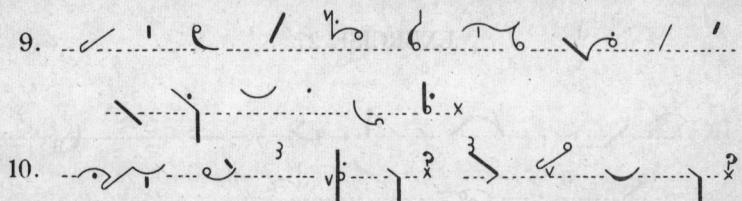

23. Final *s* circle is used to represent the word *us* in the phrases ⟨⟩ *for us* ⟨⟩ *to us* ⟨⟩ *give us* ⟨⟩ *take us* ⟨⟩ *show us* ⟨⟩ *making us* ⟨⟩ *charge us*, etc.

NOTE: ⟨⟩ *with us* ⟨⟩ *when is* ⟨⟩ *when is the* ⟨⟩ *what is* ⟨⟩ *what is the*

EXERCISE 28

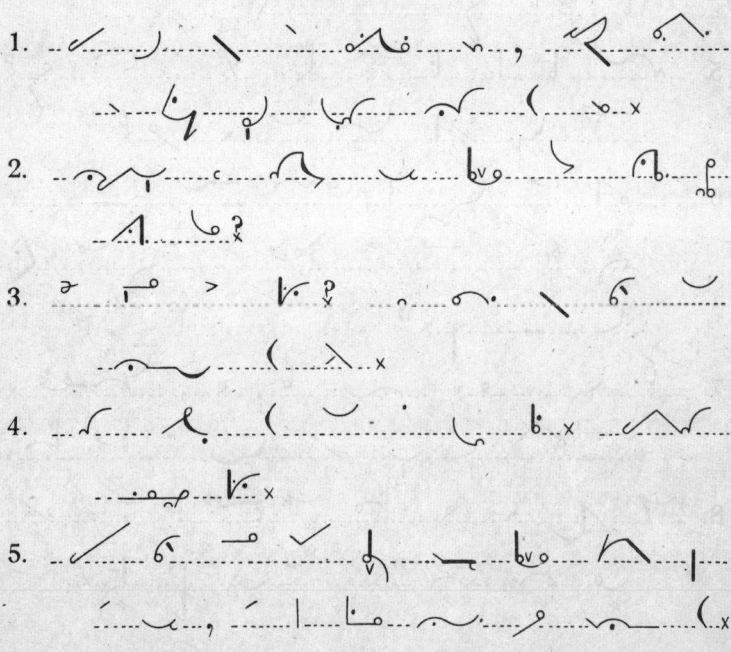

PITMAN SHORTHAND 41

[Shorthand exercises numbered 6 through 16]

24. The *s* circle is written on the outside of the angle formed by two straight strokes:

desk discuss dispose besides opposite justice sixty succeed receipt history

25. The circle at the beginning of a word represents *s* only.

In the few words beginning with *z*, the stroke *z* is used:

zeal zero zenith

EXERCISE 29

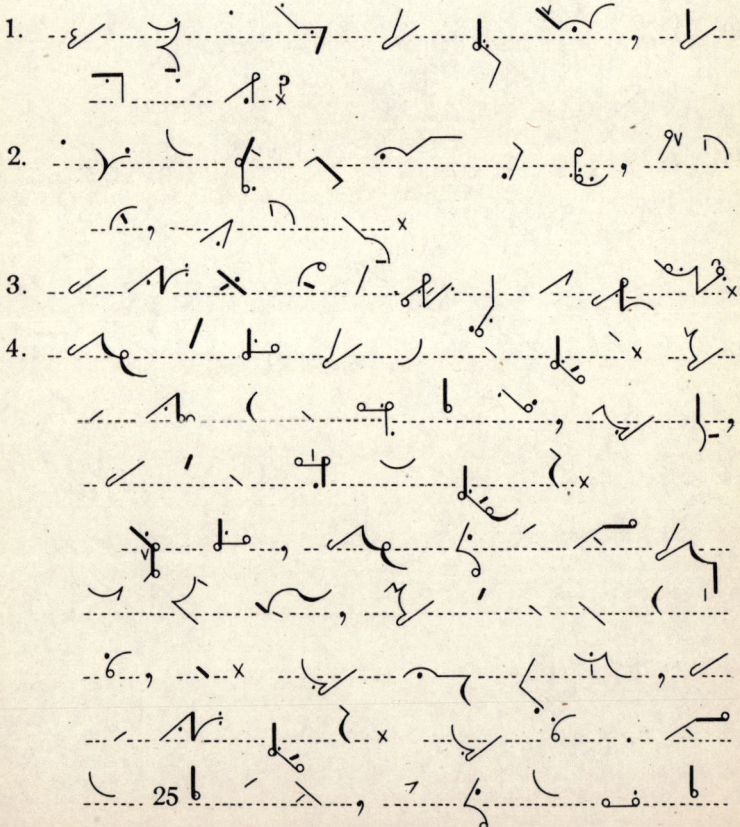

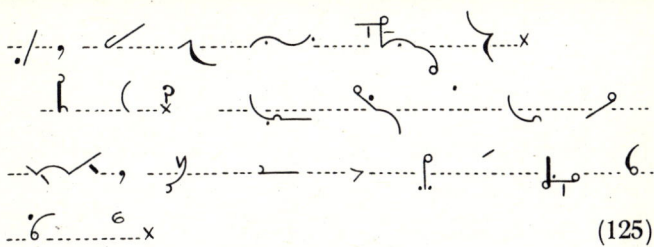

(125)

26. Although the words do not end with a vowel, upward *r* is used following the curve and circle in words like

officer　answer　sincere

27. The stroke *l* may easily be written downward, and when it is attached to the *s* circle it is written in the same direction as the circle:

vessel　nicely　cancel　council
lesson　listen　noiseless　muscle

EXERCISE 30

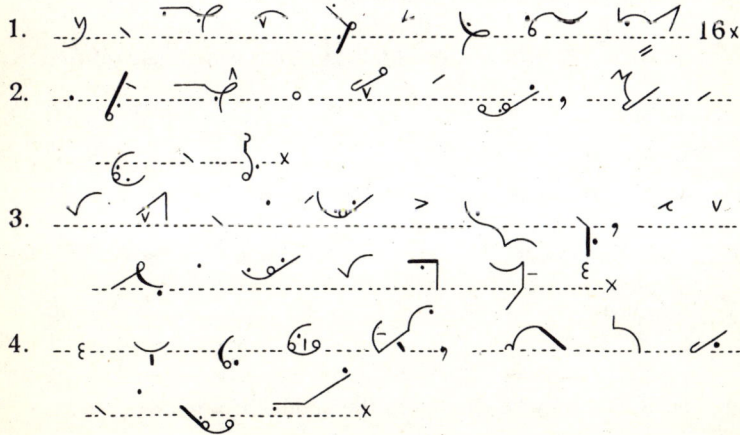

CHAPTER IX

28. *St* Loop

(*a*) A small loop, written in the same direction as the *s* circle, represents *st* (called "stee"):

fast, missed, must, honest, assist, list, invoiced, announced

stuff, style, steel, still, stone, stem, store

post, based, test, just, adjust, suggest, fixed, guest, or guessed, cost, waste, rest, haste, host

step, state, stayed, stage, stock, story

(*b*) The *st* loop represents either a light or heavy final sound:

past, paused, used, advised, refused, disposed, supposed

Final *s* circle after a *st* loop is added as shown:

lists, posts, tests, wastes, adjusts, costs, suggests

(*c*) The *st* loop may be written in the middle of a word:

testing, adjusting, suggesting

PITMAN SHORTHAND

SHORT FORMS

first   most   influence   influenced   next   all   though

NOTE: although   all right   already   always   almost   also   as fast as

EXERCISE 31

Distinctive Outlines: cost   caused

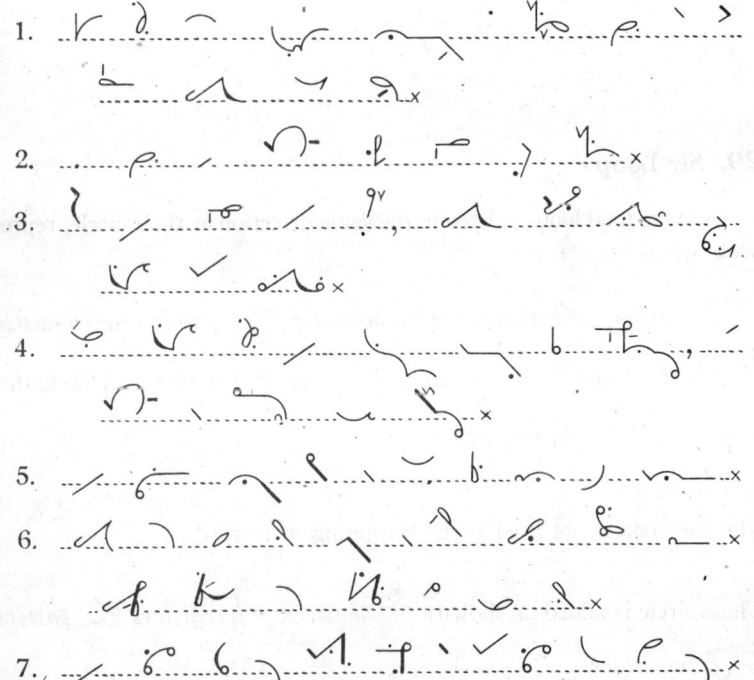

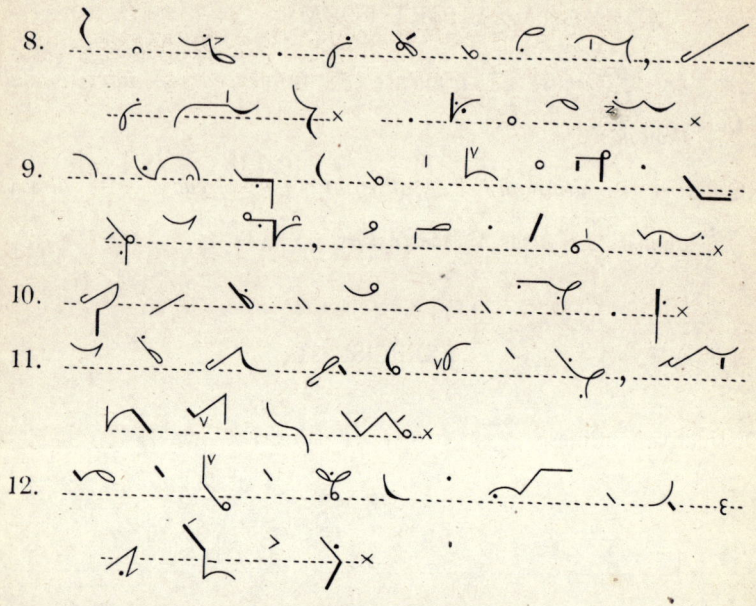

29. *Str* Loop

A large final loop, written in the same direction as the *s* circle, represents *ster:*

master   register   semester   poster   minister   administer   investor   Hester   Chester   Rochester   coaster   roadster

The *ster* loop is not used at the beginning of a word.

The *s* circle is added as shown: masters   registers   posters   investors

EXERCISE 32

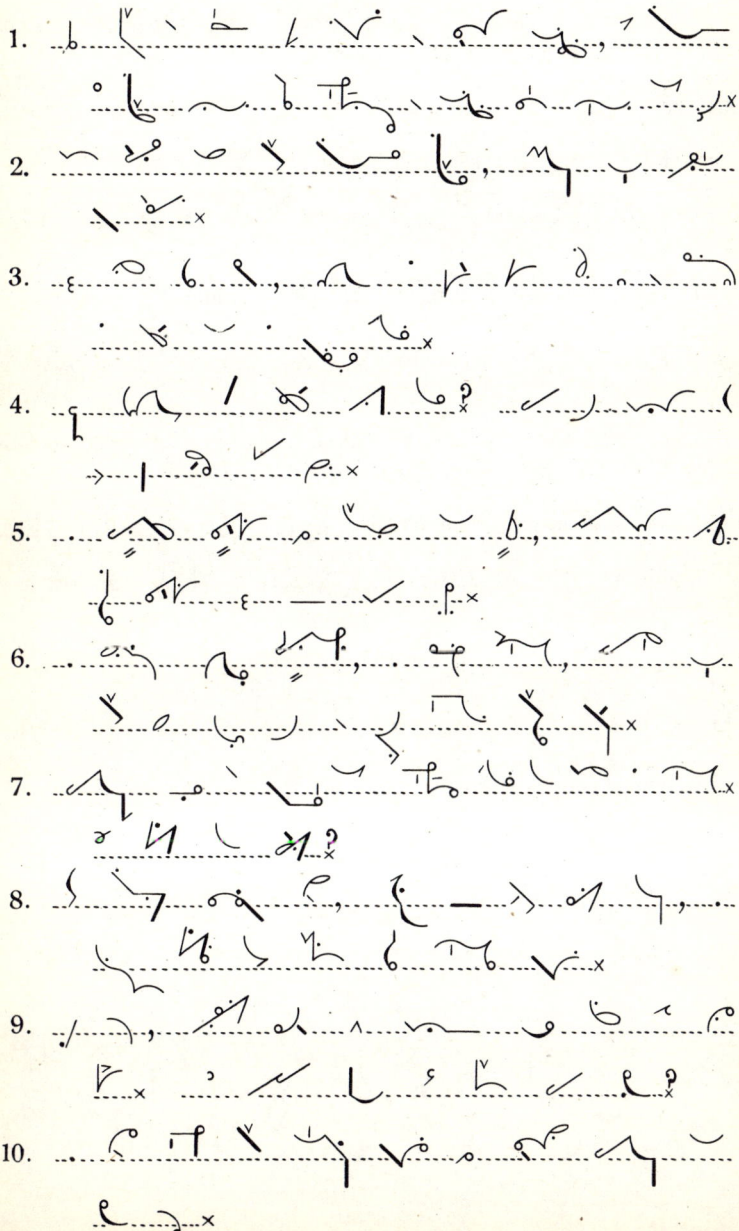

30. Ses Circle

(a) A large final circle represents *ses*, or *sez*. This large circle is written in the same direction as the circle *s*:

faces   losses   services   cases   pieces
boxes   taxes   success   passes   fixes
causes   uses   chooses   supposes

(b) The large circle also represents *ses* in the middle of a word:

necessary   necessity   successive   successfully

(c) Any vowel other than short *ĕ* between the two *s*'s is indicated by writing the vowel sign inside the circle:

basis   insist   exhaust   resist   census   Texas
Kansas   Mississippi   exercise   exercises

SHORT FORMS

themselves   ourselves   as is   is as   myself
himself   itself   much

EXERCISE 33

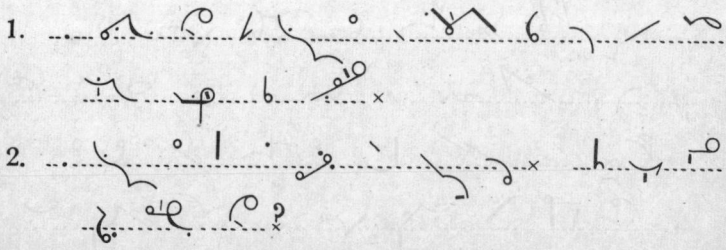

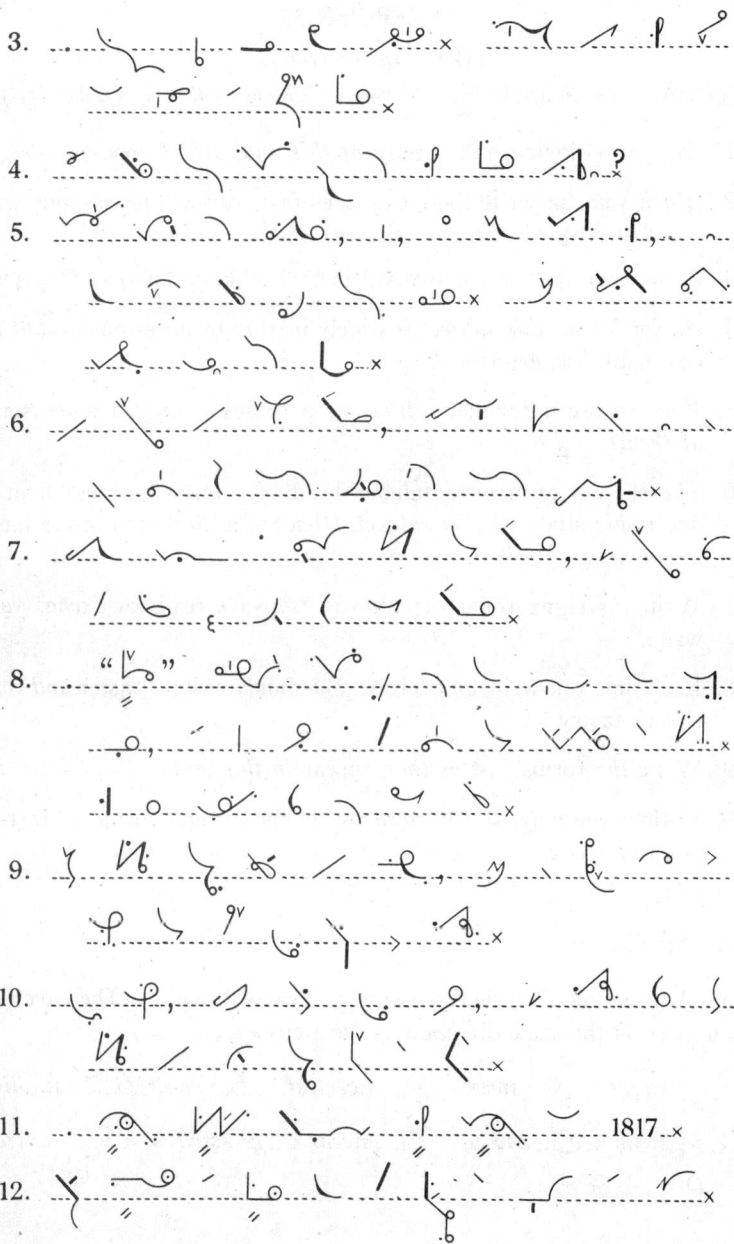

EXERCISE 34

(Write in Shorthand)

(*Phrases are indicated by hyphens. Short Forms are indicated by italic type.*)

1. *Are-you* enjoying *your* study *of-this subject? I*-hope-*you-are.*

2. *When you-can* write these exercises fast, *you*-will-*be on-your* way *to*-making *your* living *in a* business office.

3. *But* outside *of-its* value *to-you, I*-hope-*you* like-*the subject for-itself.*

4. *As you* know, *this subject is* widely used *in* business offices, *but it-has* many uses besides *this.*

5. *You-can* use *it for*-many *different* purposes. *Can-you* name some *of-them?*

6. *The* success *of*-many *a* famous head *of a large* business firm *is* due *to-his* study *of-this subject. It-was-the first* step *in-his* business career.

7. Write-*the* signs *as*-fast-*as you-can. Al*ways read back *what you*-write.

8. Each time *you*-write *an* exercise *you-should* write *it* faster *and* read *it* back faster.

9. Write-*the* forms just-*as they* appear *in-this* text.

10. *In*-time *you*-may, if-*you wish*, write these same forms *as*-fast-*as you-can speak.*

31. Sw Circle

(*a*) A large initial circle represents *sw* (called "sway"). The *sw* circle is written in the same direction as the *s* circle:

sweep sweet sweetest swell swelling
swim swing swear switch swiftest
swayed

PITMAN SHORTHAND 51

(b) The *sw* circle is used to represent the words *as we* in the phrases *as we have*, *as we think*, *as we shall*, *as we wish*, *as we may*, *as we know*, *as we can*, *as we are*, etc. It is also used to form the phrase *as well as*.

(c) The large circle is used to represent the two *s's* in the phrases *this is*, *this is the*, *this city*, *as soon as*, *as soon as possible*.

SHORT FORMS

United States, *United States of America*, *New York*, *largest*

EXERCISE 35

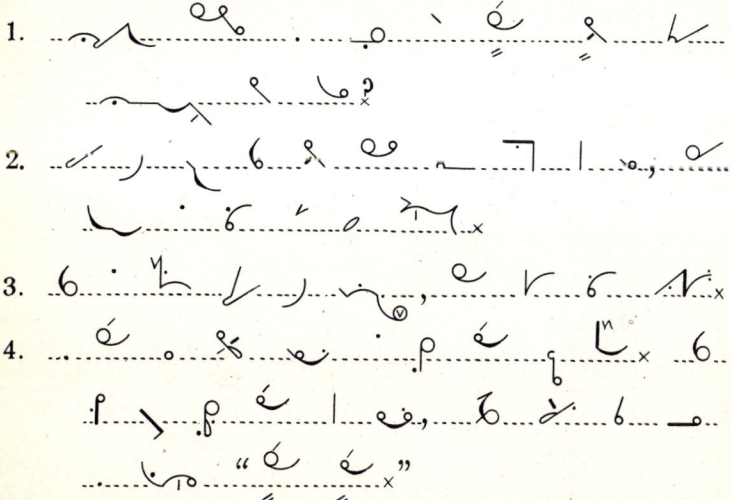

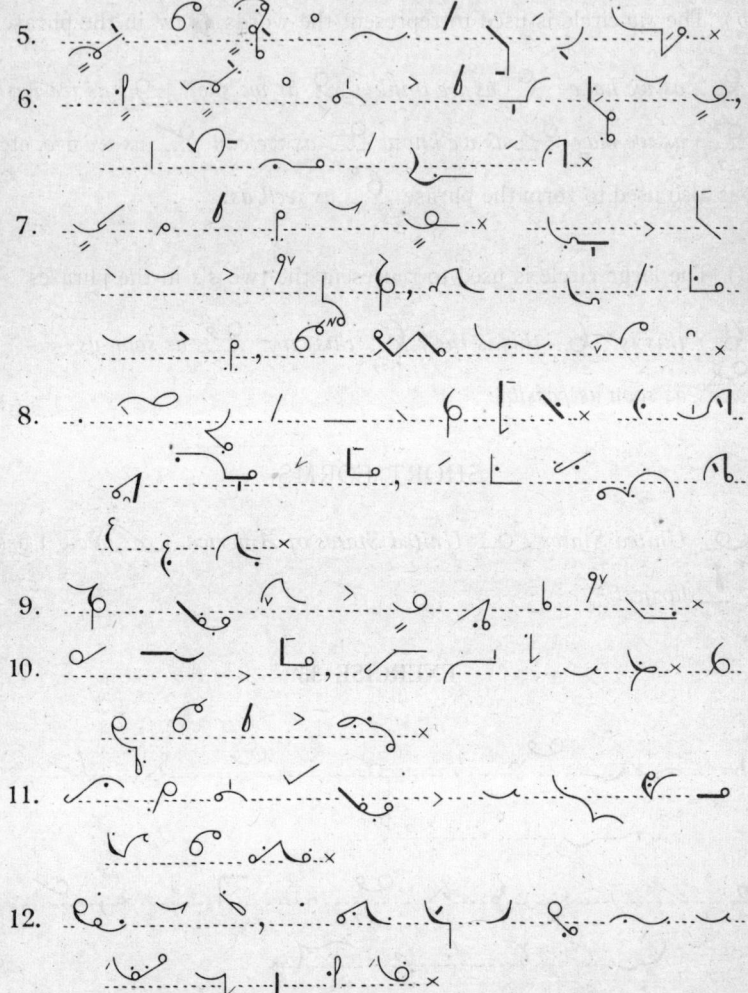

32. Vowel Indication

(a) A circle or loop is always read first at the beginning of a word. If a vowel begins a word, we must write a stroke in order to place the initial vowel sign:

sack but ask, sleep but asleep, sum but assume, scope but escape, side but aside

(b) A circle or loop is always read last at the end of a word. If a word ends in a vowel, we must write a stroke in order to place the final vowel sign:

bees but busy, police but policy, honest but honesty, lace but lazy, modest but modesty

(c) If a vowel occurs between *s* and *t*, the *st* loop is not used:

deposed but deposit, vast but visit, opposed but opposite, best but beset, rest but recite

The outline thus indicates the presence or absence of a vowel sound.

(d) As there are no places alongside a circle or loop for placing vowel signs, we must write

us, so, say, says, see, sees, seas, seize, or cease, seized or ceased, seizes or ceases, ice, essay, eyes, ease, easy, owes

Special phrases: so much, too much, how much, as much as, inasmuch as, as much as possible, as early as possible, as far as possible

SHORT FORMS

especial or *especially*   *language* or *owing*   *young*
anything   *nothing*   *something*

NOTE: In Pitman Shorthand we represent all the consonants we hear in the words we write. Except for the "short forms", where for the sake of extreme brevity we use only one or two of the consonants in a word, we do not resort to the expedient of writing only some part of a word. This is one of the reasons for the remarkable legibility of Pitman Shorthand.

As we proceed we will find that the various abbreviating devices of the system enable us to represent all the consonants in words in concise, legible, and rapid shorthand forms. These outlines are so clearly distinctive that it is unnecessary to insert the vowel signs. The outlines are perfectly legible without them.

In addition to writing a full outline of the consonants, we employ a means of indicating the presence or absence of a vowel with practically every abbreviating device of the system, and also we have position writing, which is an expedient highly prized by the fastest and most accurate shorthand writers in the world. It is not surprising, therefore, that the system is so legible.

From now on, we will omit the vowel signs in the sentences and letters, and we will speed on our way writing the outlines just as they appear in the text. You will note that we insert a vowel sign occasionally, to eliminate any possibility of hesitation in reading back your notes.

EXERCISE 36

EXERCISE 37

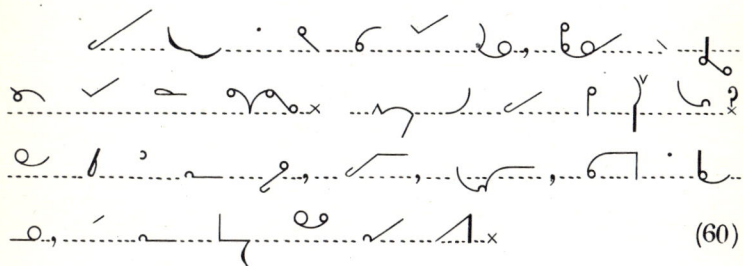

(60)

EXERCISE 38

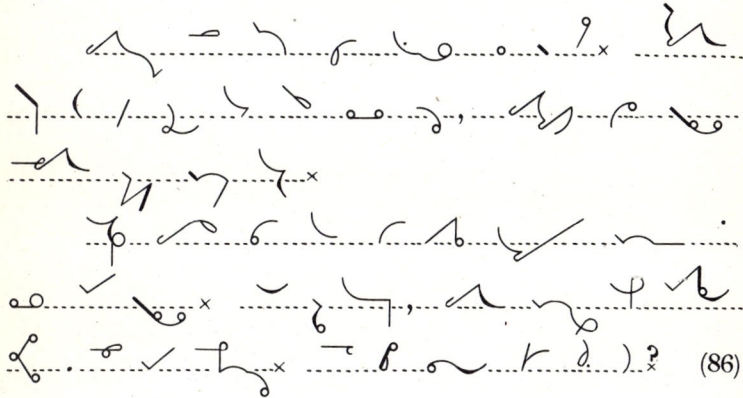

(86)

EXERCISE 39

1. (47)

2.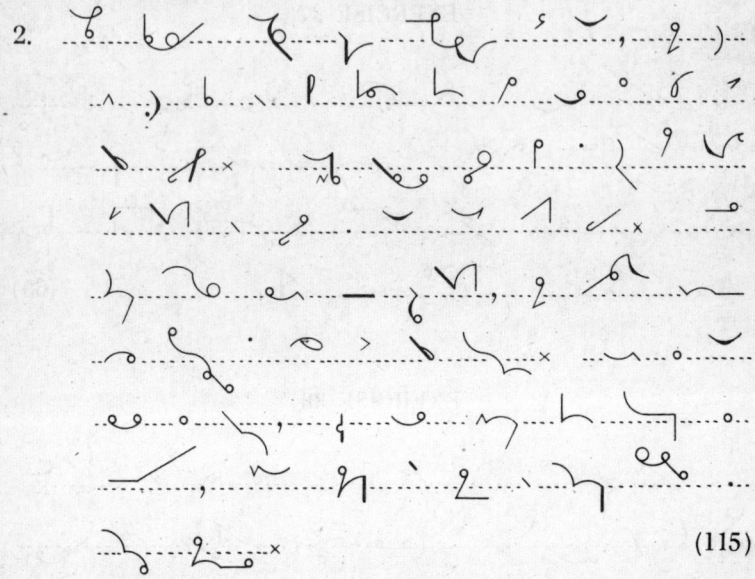
(115)

EXERCISE 40

(*Write in Shorthand*)

1. Suppose some big customer *of-yours* ceased *to*-deal-*with-you*. *What- would you do?* *We-think-you would* write *to-him,* asking if-*he had any special* reason *for-his* silence.

2. *This-is what we-are*-now asking-*you*. Although *in-the* past *our* business *with-you in-this*-city *was* extensive, *several* months *have* elapsed since *you* last *had any* dealings *with*-us. *We would* like *to* know *why, as-we-are* unaware *of any* failure *to-give-you-the* best service.

3. *We-are* always desirous *of*-satisfying *all-our* customers, *large* buyers or small. *We* assure-*you we-shall-do* anything *we-can* to put things right, if-*you think our* service *in-any*-way faulty. (119)

EXERCISE 41

(Write in Shorthand)

1. *I-have*-seen *your* notice *in to*day's "Star", *and-I should*-like *to-have* details *of-your* new Masters' Reading Series. *I-think* such *a* series *should* make *a* wide appeal, *and-I-wish-you much* success *with-it*.

2. Many *of-those who have*-seen my set *of* "Stories *of-the* Earth, Sea, *and* Sky" *speak* highly *of-it, and-several, I*-know, *have* bought similar sets *for-themselves*.

3. *I*-am-sorry *you have* allowed "Poster Designing" *to*-go out *of* stock. Such *a* book, *it*-seems *to-me, should-have a large* sale, *as* so-many *are*-now taking-up-*the* study *of-this-subject. In*-view *of-this,* may *I* suggest *a* new issue? (116)

CHAPTER X

33. Halving

Strokes are halved to indicate a following *t* or *d*.

(*a*) In words of one syllable a light stroke is halved to indicate a following *t*:

not, note, aunt, act, caught, coat, cut, met, meet, fat, fight, thought, art, wait, yet, lot, light, slight, late, let, stopped, asked, talked, kept, reached, shipped, marked, left, checked

NOTE: night

The *s* circle is always read last: notes, acts, thoughts, lots, waits, nights

(*b*) In words of one syllable a heavy stroke is halved to indicate a following *d*:

bad, bed, died, dead, God, good, loved, charged, lived, changed

SHORT FORMS

quite, could, that, without, sent, wished

EXERCISE 42

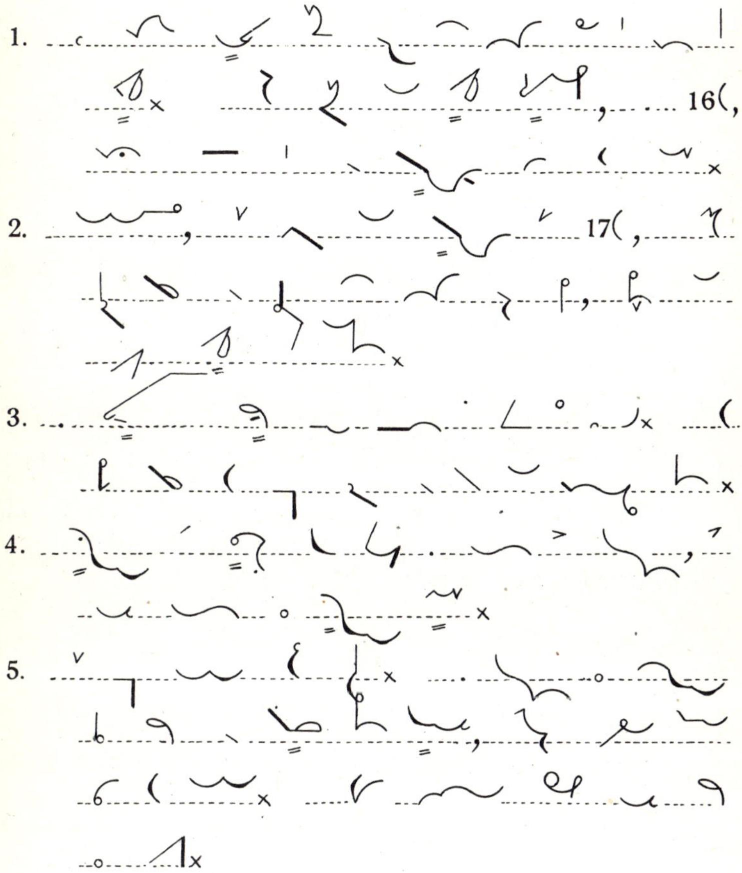

1. ...

2. ...

3. ...

4. ...

5. ...

EXERCISE 43

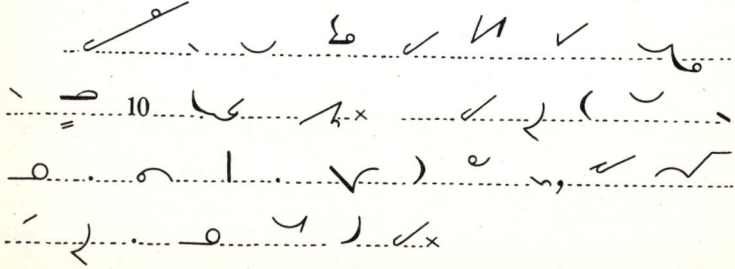

(67)

34. (*a*) In words of two or more syllables, a stroke is halved to indicate a following *t* or *d*:

(1) attached   answered   except   suggested   avoid   market   recent   absent   admit   arrived   engaged   enjoyed   estate   stated   exact   result   benefit   booklet

(2) actually   writing   badly   lately   entire   entirely   evidence   sometimes   waiting   certain   goodbye   absolutely

(3) omit   omitted   note   noted   accept   accepted   submit   submitted   await   awaited   limit   limited   visit   visited   list   listed   remit   remitted   deduct   deducted   notify   notified   invited

(*b*) A half length stroke is not written through the line to indicate a third position. Words like the following are written on the line:

east   feet   fit   sheets   bid   did   written   invite   indeed   needed   instead   little   moved   Pittsburgh

(c) Where a final diphthong is joined, a stroke is halved fo indicate a final *t* or *d:*

doubt   about   bowed   cute   issued

EXERCISE 44

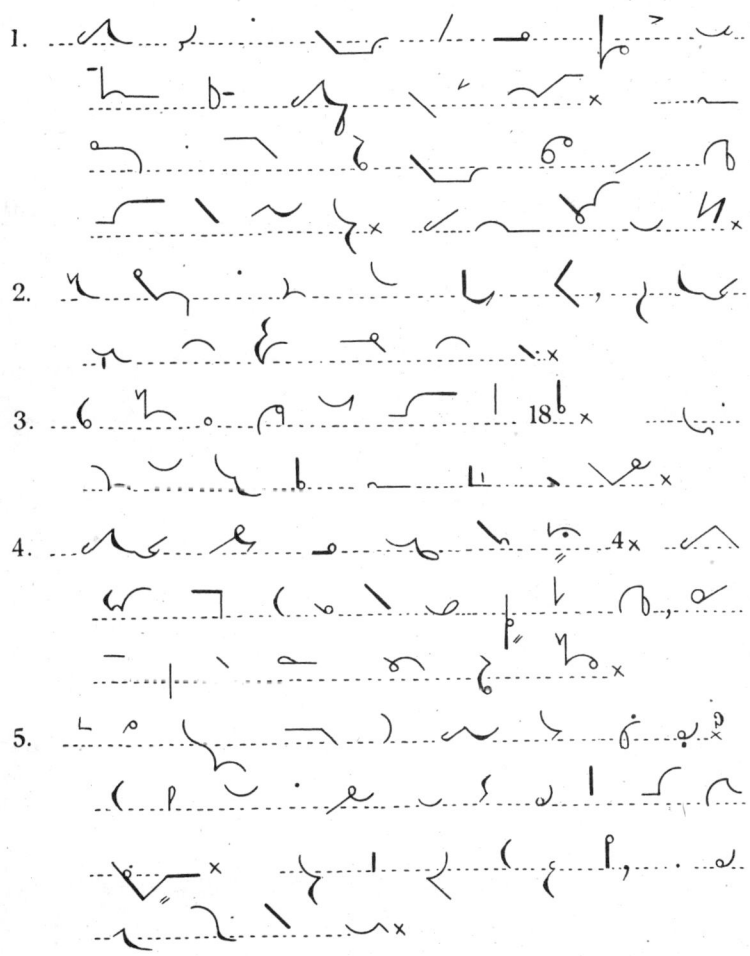

EXERCISE 45

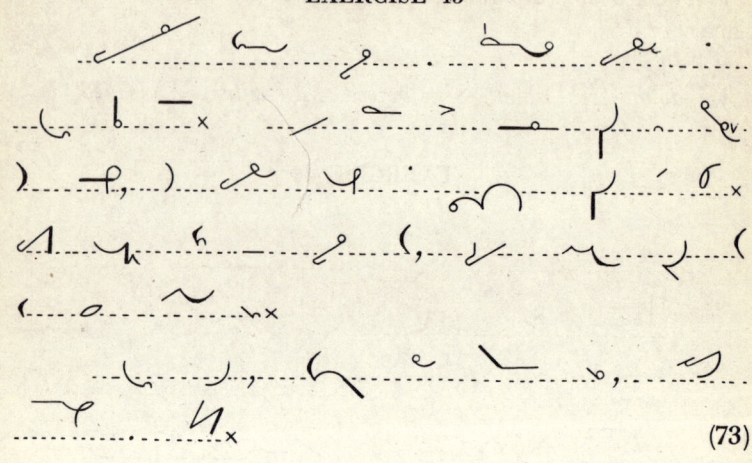

(73)

EXERCISE 46

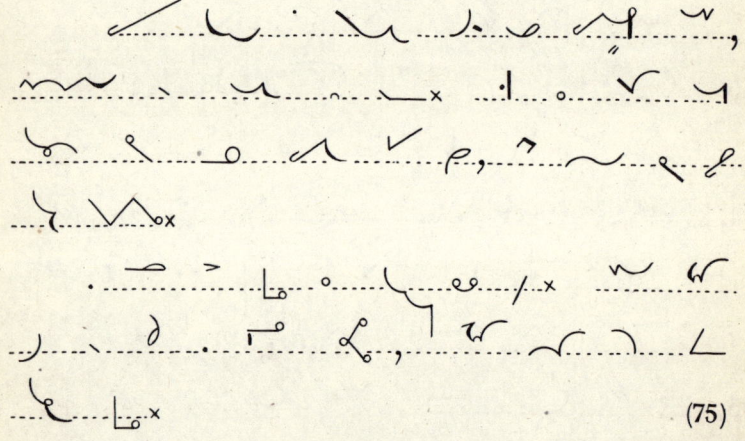

(75)

EXERCISE 47

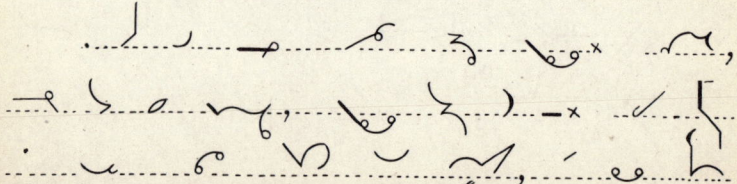

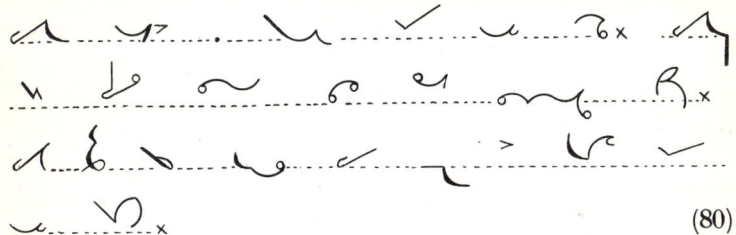

(80)

EXERCISE 48
(*Write in Shorthand*)

1. Little by little *all of*-us form habits. Sometimes *we* form good habits, *and*-sometimes *our* habits *are* bad. *It-is* certain *that-the* habit *of* accuracy *is* likely *to-be of-the-most* value *to*-us *in a* business office. (41)

2. *We-have-sent several* notes *to-you* asking-*you* to pay-*the* bill *for-the*-goods *you* bought six-months-ago, *but-you have*-not answered any *of-them.*

   We-are-sorry *to* say *that* now *we-shall-have to*-take-*the usual* steps *to*-avoid-*the* loss *of-our* money, if-*your* check *is*-not received by-*the first of next* month. *We* urge *you to*-mail *your* check *to-us without*-delay. (74)

35. (*a*) To avoid confusion with *should* and *and,* we do not use *rt* and *rts* standing alone. Therefore we write rate, rates, right, rights, write, wrote, route

(*b*) In certain words, where the proper length of a halved stroke would not clearly show, the halving principle is not employed: fact, effect, liked, locate, minute, select, territory, tonight

64 NEW STANDARD COURSE

(ε). When a final vowel follows *t* or *d*, it is necessary to write the stroke *t* or *d* in order to place the vowel sign:

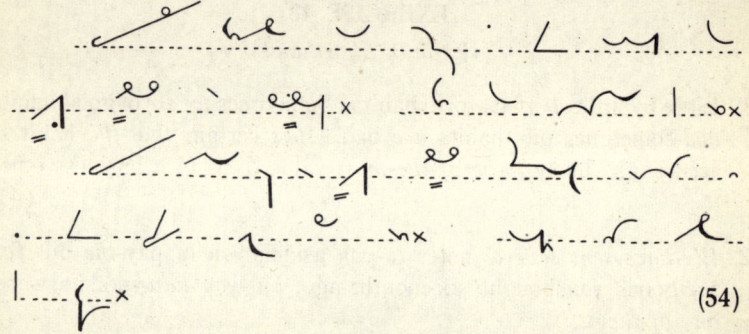

EXERCISE 49

(54)

EXERCISE 50

(64)

EXERCISE 51

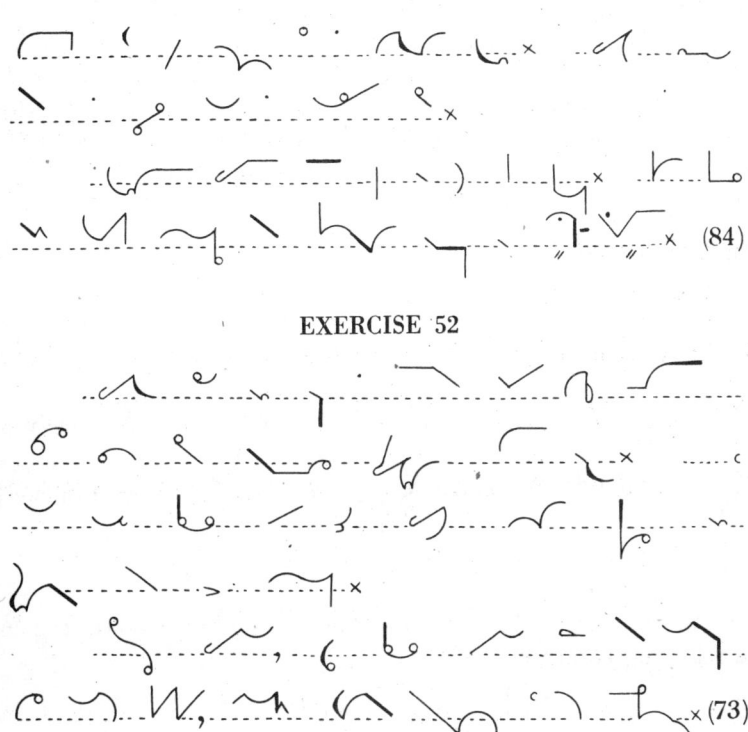

EXERCISE 53
(*Write in Shorthand*)

Do-you know *that-we* sell good tires? *It-is*-not-necessary *for-you to* buy tires now *in a* repair shop, *for our* store now carries *them*. *You-can* buy *them when you-are in-the* store, just-*as you would* select silks, or *something for-your* house.

These tires *are* good value, *and*-they sell rapidly. Each *of-them* carries *our* guarantee. (64)

EXERCISE 54
(*Write in Shorthand*)

It-is quite some time since *you* bought *anything in-this* store. *I-am*-writing *to-you* myself, because *I should-be* sorry *to*-lose *your* custom.

It-may-*be that*-*we*-*have* offended *you in*-some-way. If-*this*-*is*-*the* case, *I*-hope-*you*-will write *to*-*me*. *Our* service *and our* way *of*-*doing* business *are things which*-*we* boast about. *It*-*would*-*be a* pity *to* stay away *because of*-*something which could*-*be* easily remedied, *and you*-*should*-*not* hesitate *to*-write *to*-*me* and let-*me*-know-*the* cause. (95)

36. Downward *L*

Usually *l* is written upward.

(1) For convenience in writing, *l* is written downward after *n* or *ng*:

only   unless   until   canal   analysis   exceedingly   annual   evidently   unfortunately   recently   certainly

(2) For the purpose of vowel indication, *l* is written downward in the following two cases.

(*a*) When an initial vowel comes before *l*, and the *l* is followed by a simple horizontal stroke:

alone   along   Ellen   alike   elm   Illinois   Elmira   elect   elected   but   long   like   Lena   lake   lime

(*b*) When *l* follows *f, v, sk*, or a straight upstroke, and a vowel does not end the word:

fail   fall   awful   feel   feeling   fell   fill   full   veal   skill   rule   scale   barrel   successful   useful   Yale   rail

PITMAN SHORTHAND

When a vowel ends the word, *l* is written upward:

folly   awfully   fellow   fully   lovely
successfully   usefully   yellow   rely   sickly

NOTE. Special Outlines: volume   column   film

SHORT FORMS

inform-ed   never, November   satisfactory   respect-ed
expect-ed   inspect-ed-ion   January   February
together   altogether   insurance

EXERCISE 55

1.
2.
3.
4.
5.
6.
7.

EXERCISE 56

(145)

EXERCISE 57

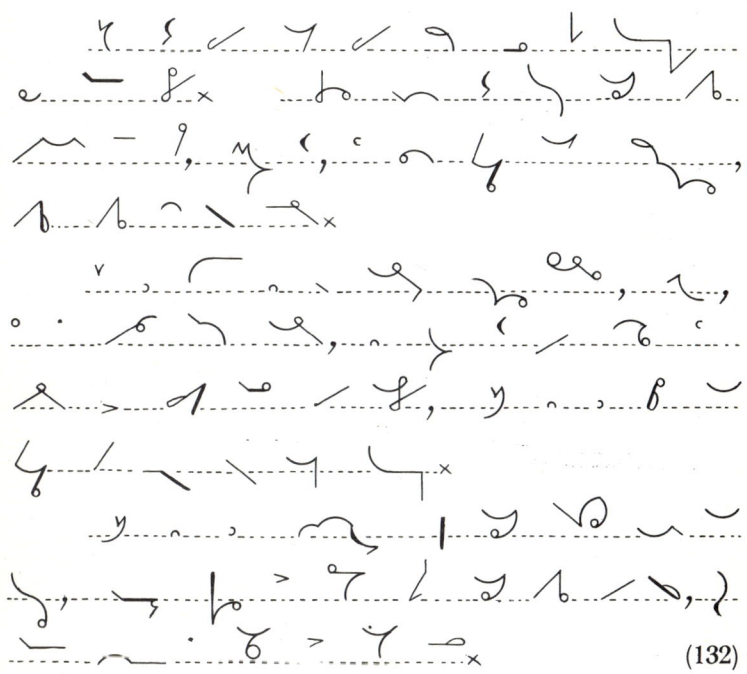

(132)

37. Abbreviated *W*

A small initial semicircle, written as shown, is used as an abbreviation for *w* at the beginning of *k, g, m,* and upward and downward *r:*

week or weak   walk   walked   wig   womanly   worry   worth   worthy   were   wear   wire   work   worked   worse   worst

NOTE: The small semicircle is always read first. When a vowel begins a word, the stroke *w* must be written:

awake   awoke   aware

Special Phrases: you were   which were   who were   they were   we were

EXERCISE 58

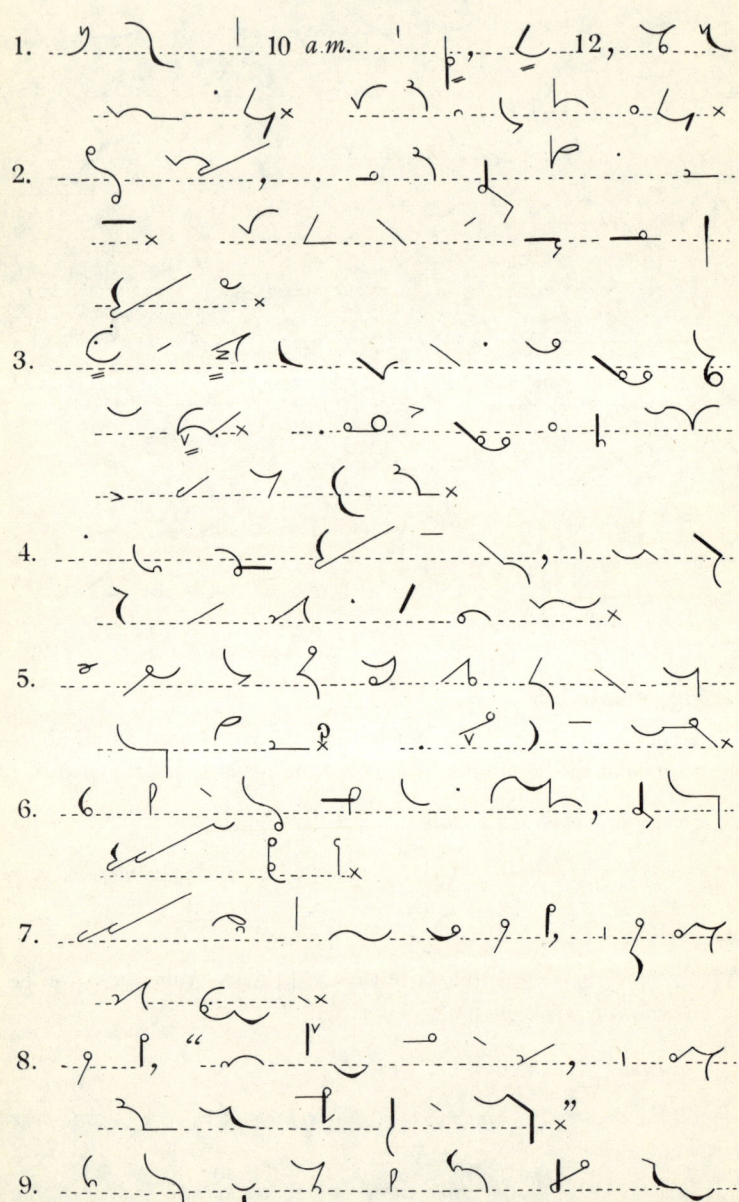

PITMAN SHORTHAND

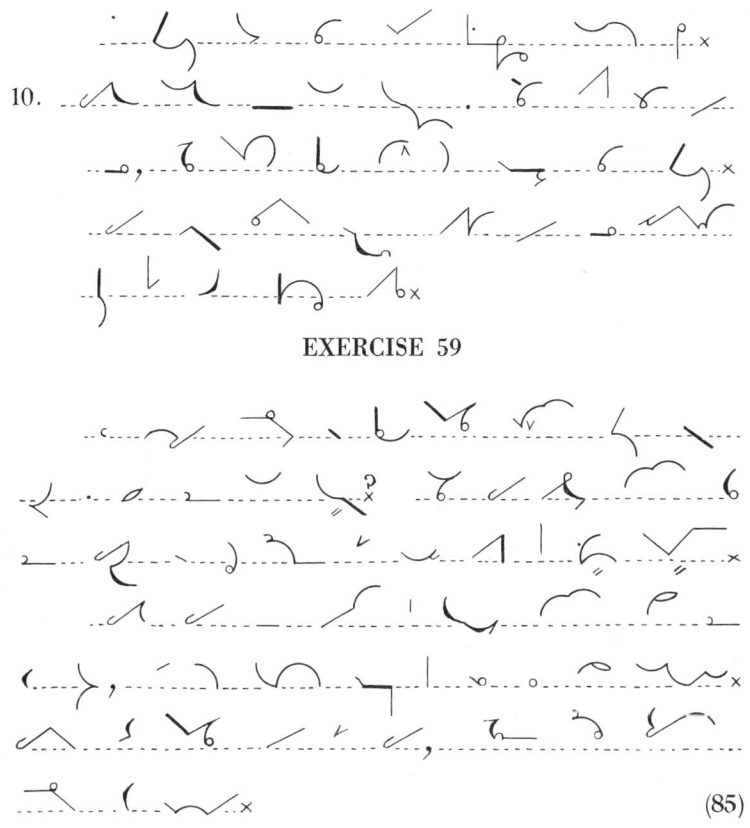

10.

EXERCISE 59

(85)

EXERCISE 60
(*Write in Shorthand*)

I-wish to-thank-you for-the catalog *which-you-*were good-enough *to-*mail *to-me* recently. *Several* books listed *on* page 21 appear *to-be* just *what I-*am looking *for. I-have* marked *them on-the* attached sheet.

*Although I-think that-*these books *should-be* useful *to-me in-*my work, *I would* like *to inspect them to* see if-they *would-be satisfactory. Can any of-the* books *be sent* back *to-you* if, *when I-have* looked at-*them, I-*decide *that-*they *would-*not-*be satisfactory for-*my purpose? (96)

CHAPTER XI

38. Double Consonants – *Pl Series*

A small beginning hook, written on the circle side of straight downstrokes and *k* and *g*, forms a series of double consonants:

pl   bl   tl   dl   chl   jl   kl   gl

These double consonants are called *pel, bel,* etc. They are pronounced as a single sound (pl-a, play), and the vowel signs are placed to them just as they are placed to single consonants.

play   place   places   placing   placed
replace   plate   played   plus   blue   black
blame   blank   block   class   clear   clerk
close   closed   enclose   cloth   clothes   club
claim   glass   glad
apply   applied   replied   simple   couple   able
enable   double   table   reasonable   terrible
oblige   total   entitled   include   included
including   local   uncle   article   single
duplicate   o'clock

Distinctive Forms: valuable   available

An *s* circle at the beginning is written inside the hook of the *pl* series:

supply   supplied   split   settle   settled
possible   possibly   displace   disclose   physical
exclusive

SHORT FORMS

people   belief, believe, or believed   tell   till   deliver, delivered, or delivery   call   called   equal, equally   equaled, or cold   building, or able-to

Phrases: at all   by all   I believe

EXERCISE 61

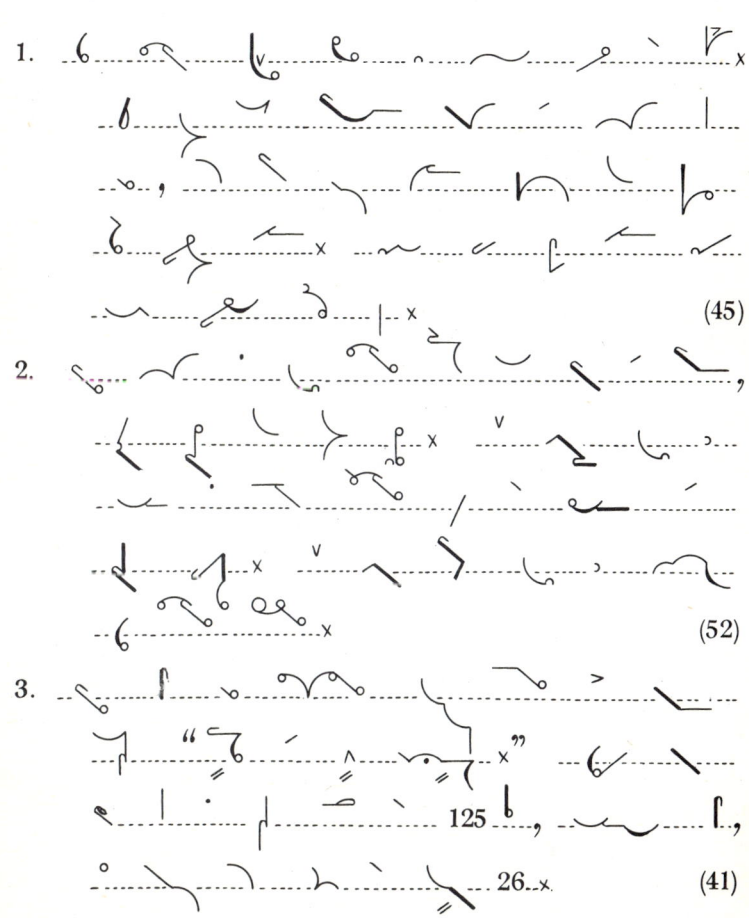

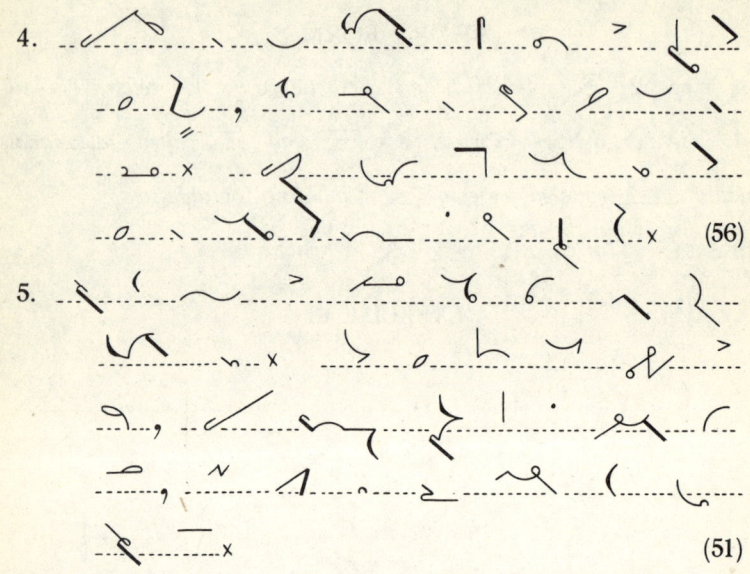

EXERCISE 62

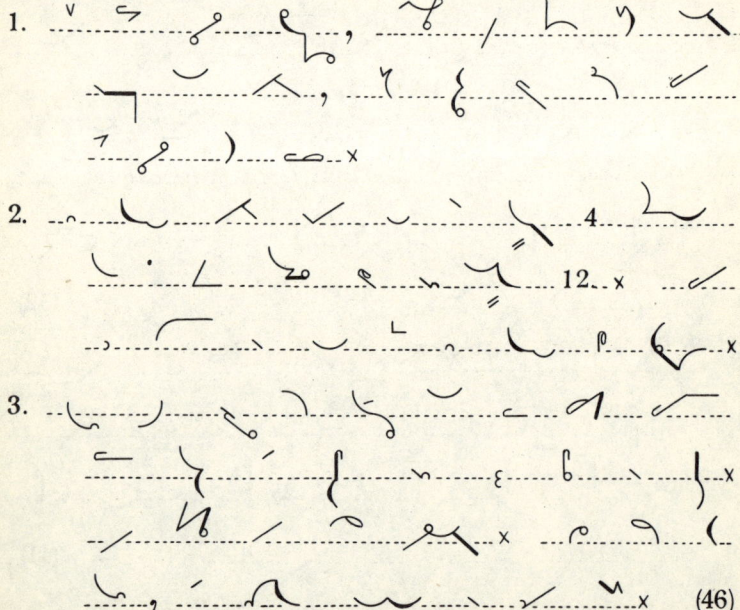

4. (66)

5. (40)

EXERCISE 63

27 (111)

EXERCISE 64

(Write in Shorthand)

We-enclose *a* booklet *which gives* details *of-our* plate-glass window *insurance*. *When-you* renew *your insurance we-believe it*-will pay *you to*-take-out *this* type *of* policy.

You-will-note *that-we-are* able-to give-you *especially* useful service. *As*-soon-*as-we* receive *your* claim *we* replace-*the* glass. *Your* claim *is* settled *without*-delay, *and a* check *large* enough *to* pay *for all-the* damage, including *any* damage *to-your* window display, *is* sent *to-you*.

If-*you wish*, *we-shall-be-glad to-have* somebody *call on-you to-tell-you anything you*-may *wish to* know about *this insurance*. (108)

39. Double Consonants – *Pr* Series

A small initial hook, written on the non-circle side of straight downstrokes and *k* and *g,* forms a series of double consonants:

pr   br   tr   dr   chr   jr   kr   gr

These double consonants are called *per, ber,* etc.

(a) pray press price propose presume present April break branch bridge bring bright broke brought try trial trip truly trust trusting dry drop dream dress address grow group greatest grades across crop cream cry credit crowd

PITMAN SHORTHAND

(b) *better* *labor* *teacher* *manager* *proceed* *progress* *properly* *increased* *program* *problem* *proud* *degree* *agreed* *daughter* *water* *withdraw* *practical* *liberal* *graduate* *October*

SHORT FORMS

Dr., doctor *dear* *during* *truth* *principal, principally,* or *principle* *liberty* *member, remember,* or *remembered* *number,* or *numbered* *care*

EXERCISE 65

1.

2. 87⁵⁰ 463 16 85⁵⁰ (65)

3. 16 463 (42)

4.

(49)

EXERCISE 66

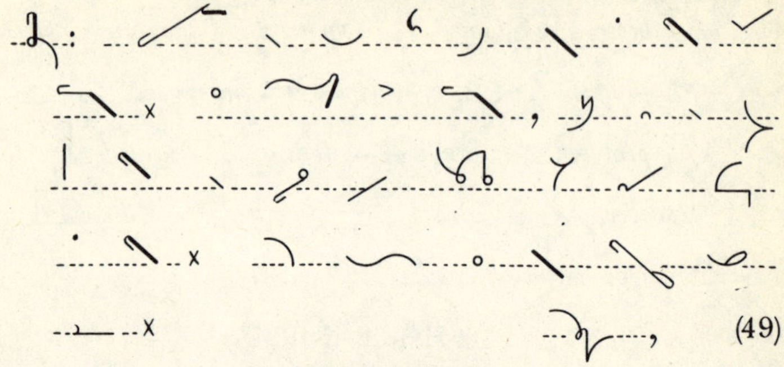

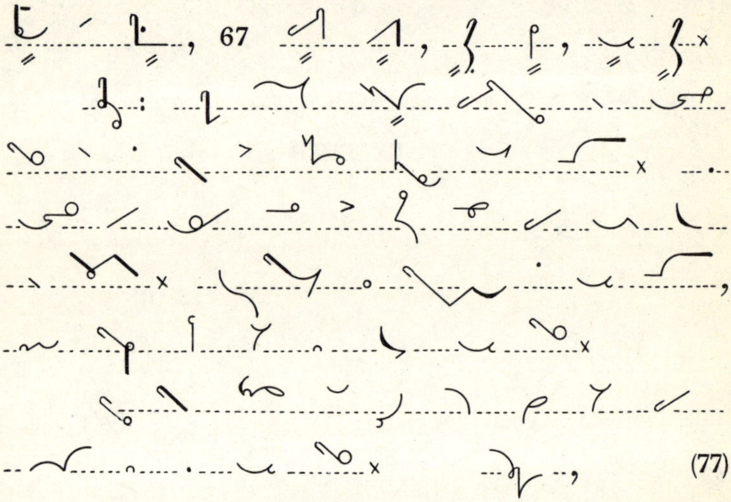

(77)

EXERCISE 67

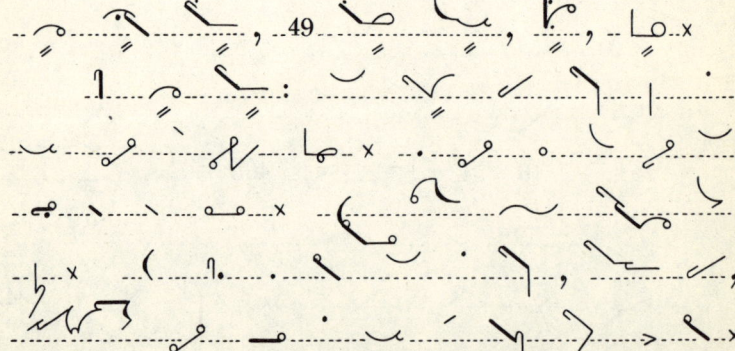

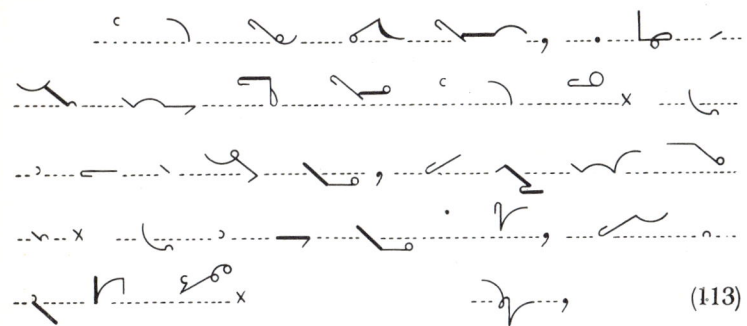

(113)

EXERCISE 68
(*Write in Shorthand*)

Dr. Thomas Waters, 21 Bridge Avenue, Cincinnati, Ohio

Dear Dr. Waters: *We*-are taking-*the liberty of* asking-*you* to address *our* graduates at *our* exercises *on* January 29. *Our principal and* teachers, *as*-well-*as*-*the* graduates, *would-be* proud *to*-*have*-*you* deliver *an* address. *As*-*the principal* speaker *on*-*our* program *we*-know-*that what*-*you*-*would* tell-*us* *would-be* remembered *by*-*all our* graduates *for*-*many*-*years to-come*.

We-know-*that*-*you have* many *calls to-speak*, *and*-*that your* time *is* exceedingly valuable, *but*-*we*-feel *that*-*you*-will-*be*-glad *to*-talk *to*-us *if*-*you* possibly *can*. *We*-trust *that*-*you*-will-*be*-able-*to* accept. *Yours*-truly,

(109)

40. (*a*) When an initial circle or loop is written on the same side as the hook of the *pr* series, the *r* is included:

spring   *strange*   *strong*   *street*   *straight*

strength   *supper*   *separate*   *secretary*   *sweeter*

sticker

(*b*) Both hook and circle are shown in the middle of a word:

extra   *extremely*   *express*

(*c*) When *skr* or *sgr* follows *t* or *d*, the combinations are written thus:

describe   *disgrace*   *disagree*

Distinctive Forms: *propriety*   *property*

propose   *purpose*

SHORT FORMS

description   *surprise*   *surprised*

EXERCISE 69

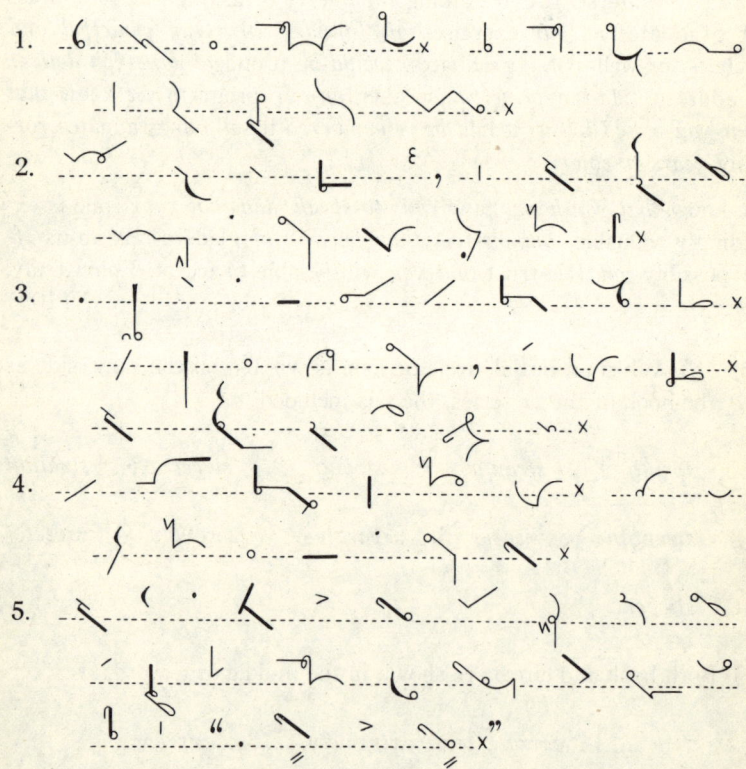

EXERCISE 70

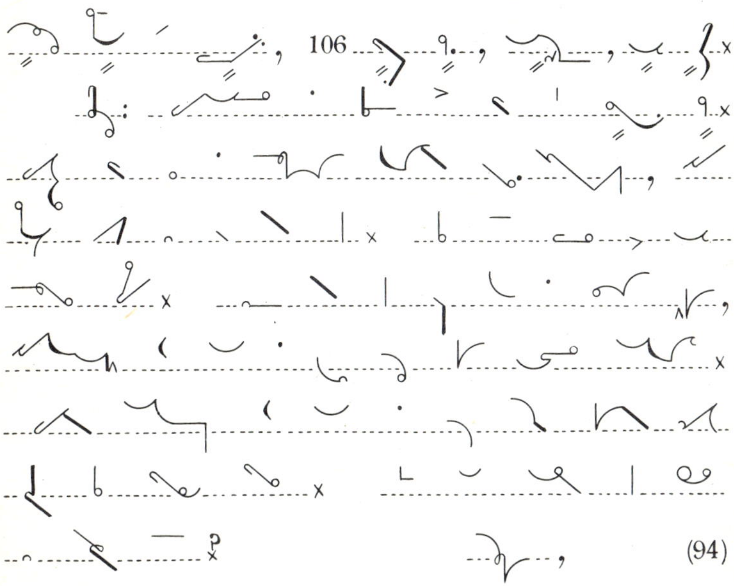

(shorthand exercise) (94)

41. Special Use of Double Consonants

In a special group of words, the double consonant strokes are used although a distinct vowel comes between a consonant and *l* or *r*. The double consonant strokes are employed in order to secure briefer or more facile outlines. The most important of these words are given below.

Although it is seldom necessary to vocalize these special outlines, a dot vowel may be indicated by writing a small circle instead of the dot, either after or before the double consonant stroke:

parcel   *darling*   *dark*   *charm*   *direct*

directly

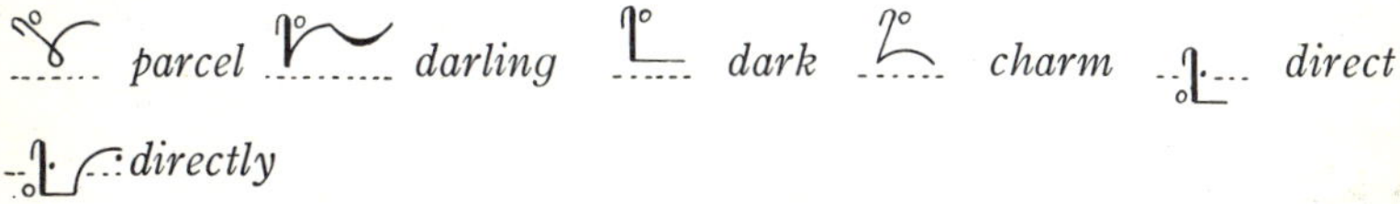

The short *ĕ* vowel is never indicated in words like *person*   *girl*

term

NEW STANDARD COURSE

A dash vowel, or a diphthong, is shown by writing the vowel sign or diphthong sign through, or at the beginning, or at the end of the stroke:

college   accordance   accordingly   course   court   church   occurred   record   purchase   correct   collect   courtesy   attorney   lecture   literature   lectures

Distinctive Forms: regard   regret

EXERCISE 71

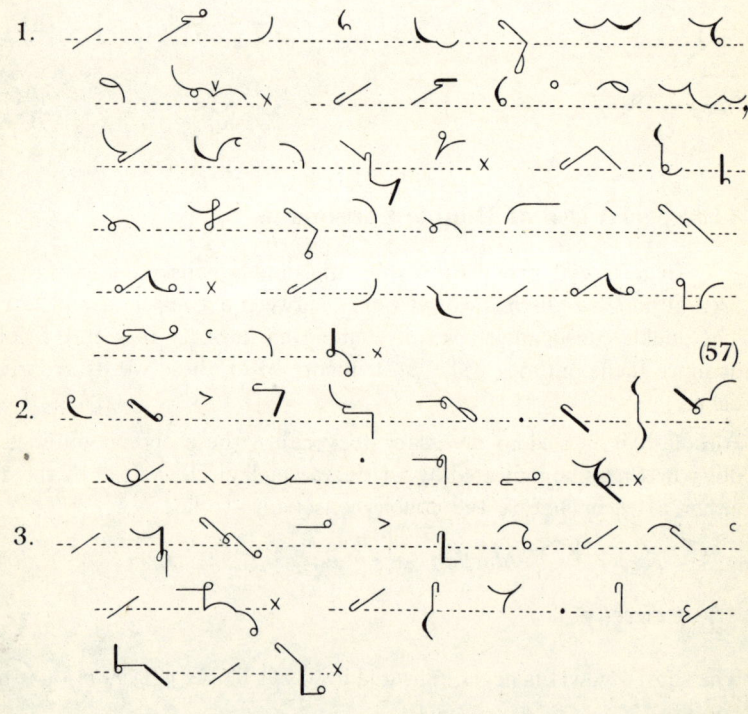

PITMAN SHORTHAND

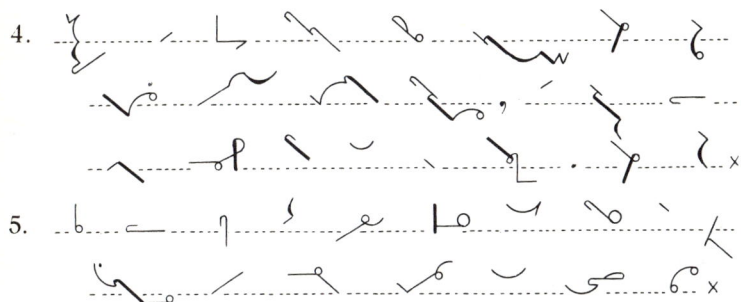

EXERCISE 72

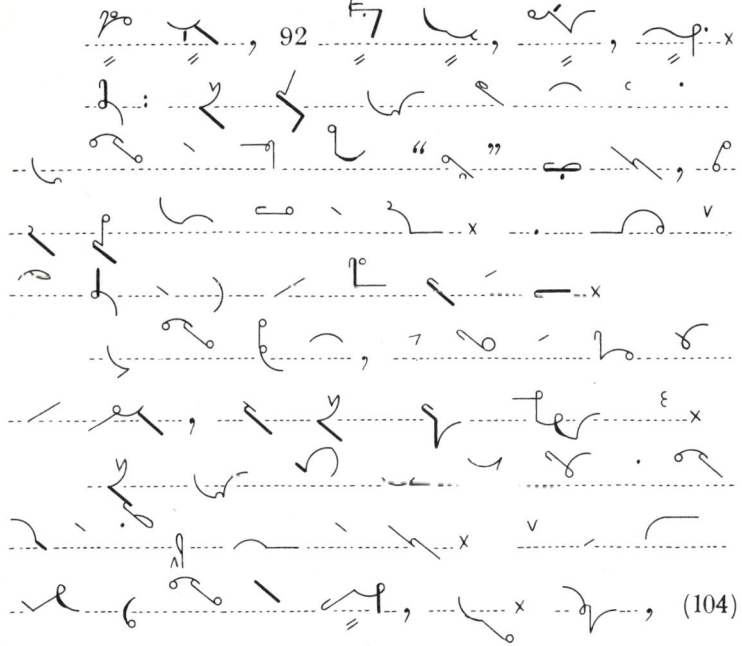

(104)

EXERCISE 73

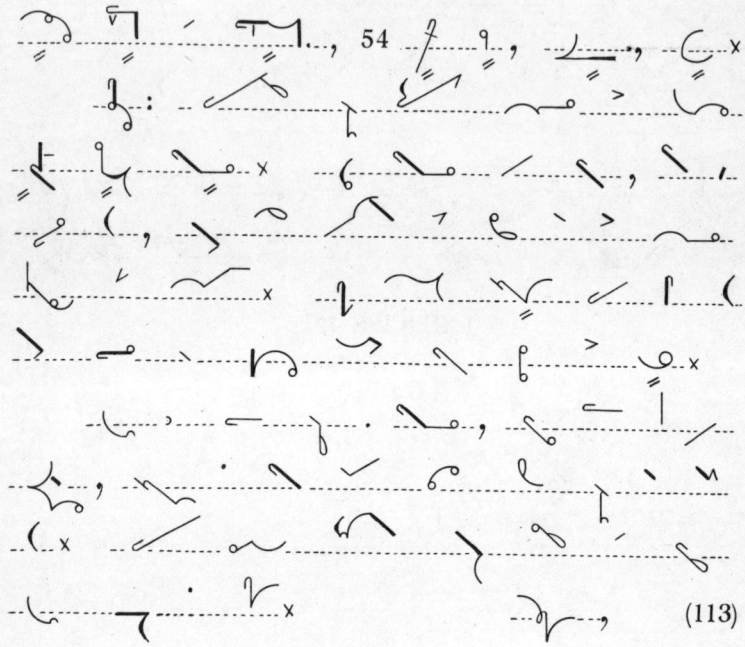

(113)

EXERCISE 74

(101)

EXERCISE 75
(Write in Shorthand)

1. If-*you*-will bring *me a* supply *of*-samples *of-this* new breakfast food, *I*-will-try *to*-close-*the* deal *with-the* firm *myself*.

2. *During-the* course *of*-my lecture, *I-shall* try *to* show *how-the* progress *of* art *is* related *to-the* growth *of* industry.

3. *When I*-know *what-the* proposed water power scheme includes, *I-shall-be*-glad *to*-express my views.

4. *A* loud voice troubles *and* annoys us. Pleasant voices resemble sweet music.

5. Castles *in-the* air *are* fabrics *which* soon crumble, *but* dreamers *have* solved many *a* pressing problem.

6. Few *people are* able *themselves to* better-*the* labor *of-those* they blame.

EXERCISE 76
(Write in Shorthand)

Peter Semple *and*-Sons, 92 Court Street, Rochester, New-York.

Dear-Sirs: Due *to-the* rapidly increasing cost *of* copper *and* steel, *we-are*-obliged *to* increase-*the* prices *of*-many *of-the* articles included *in our* catalog. *We* extremely regret-*the* necessity *of* passing *on-the* higher charges *to-our* customers, *but at*-*the* present-time *this-is-the* only possible course *we-can* follow.

You-will-*be* notified *when* better terms *are* available *on-our* supplies, *and-we-are thus* enabled *to*-reduce-*the* prices. *Yours*-truly, (79)

42. Double Consonants — *Curves*

(*a*) A small initial hook, written on the inside of curves, forms a series of double consonant strokes, *fr, vr,* etc.

Friday   afraid   average   every   everybody
other   otherwise   author   shrub   shrink
dinner   pressure   measure   leisure   enclosure
favor   favorable   favored   endeavor   honor
manner   effort   efforts   sooner   summer
farmers   nervous   corner   north   normal

(*b*) A large initial hook, written on the inside of curves, forms the double consonants *fl, vl,* etc.

fly   flat   flowers   evil   civil   arrival
approval   beautiful   delightful   final
finally   original   originally   privilege
personal   personally   travel

SHORT FORMS

nor, or in our   near   own   owner   more,
remark, or remarked   remarkable   Mr. or mere   sure
pleasure   larger   largely   everything   over
however   respectfully

EXERCISE 77

EXERCISE 78

EXERCISE 79

PITMAN SHORTHAND

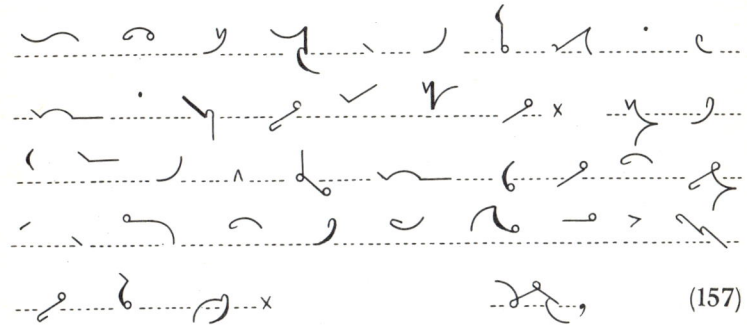

(157)

43. Additional Forms

(a) The double consonants *fr, vr, thr,* and *THr,* are represented by ⟍ *fr* ⟍ *vr* ⟍ *thr* ⟍ *THr* (reverse forms), as well as by ⟍ *fr* ⟍ *vr* ⟍ *thr* ⟍ *THr* (original forms).

When one of these double consonant strokes is the only stroke in the word, the reverse form is used *if the word does not begin with a vowel:*

⟍ *free* ⟍ *freight* ⟍ *fruit* ⟍ *three* ⟍ *through* but ⟍ *either* ⟍ *ever* ⟍ *offer* ⟍ *offered* ⟍ *other*

(b) When joined to another stroke, the forms are used which join most conveniently. Usually, the reverse forms are joined to strokes written towards the right:

⟍ *before* ⟍ *bother* ⟍ *leather* ⟍ *brother* ⟍ *cover* ⟍ *covered* ⟍ *discover* ⟍ *forgot* ⟍ *gather* ⟍ *lever* ⟍ *Denver*

NOTE: ⟍ *Thursday* ⟍ *thirty* ⟍ *fresh*

(c) After *k, g, n,* or a straight upstroke, *fl* and *vl* are reversed:

rifle   *reflect*   *naval*   *novel*   *rival*

44. The double consonant stroke *shl* is always written upward. The stroke *shr* is always written downward:

official   *shelf*   *partial*   *specialize*   *specialty*

essential   *artificial*   *pressure*   *Fisher*

45. The heavy sign is used to represent *ng-kr* or *ng-gr:*

thinker   *banker*   *conquer*   *finger*   *stronger*

SHORT FORMS

from   *very*   *they are*   *their, there*

EXERCISE 80

1.
2.
3.

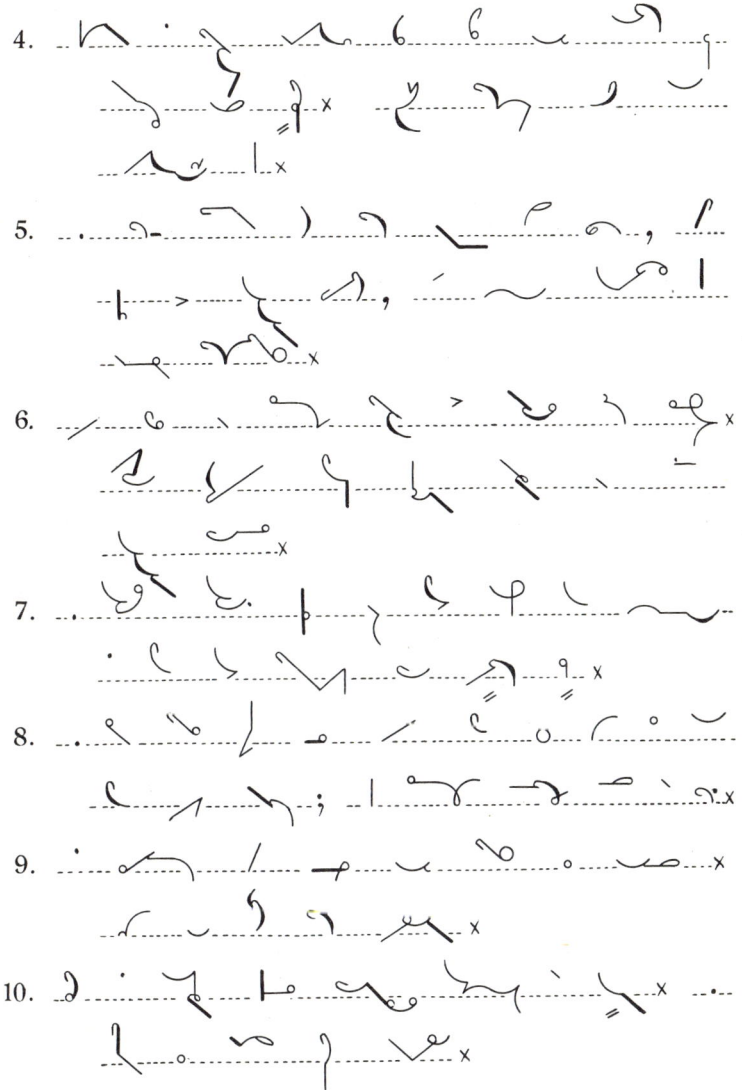

EXERCISE 81

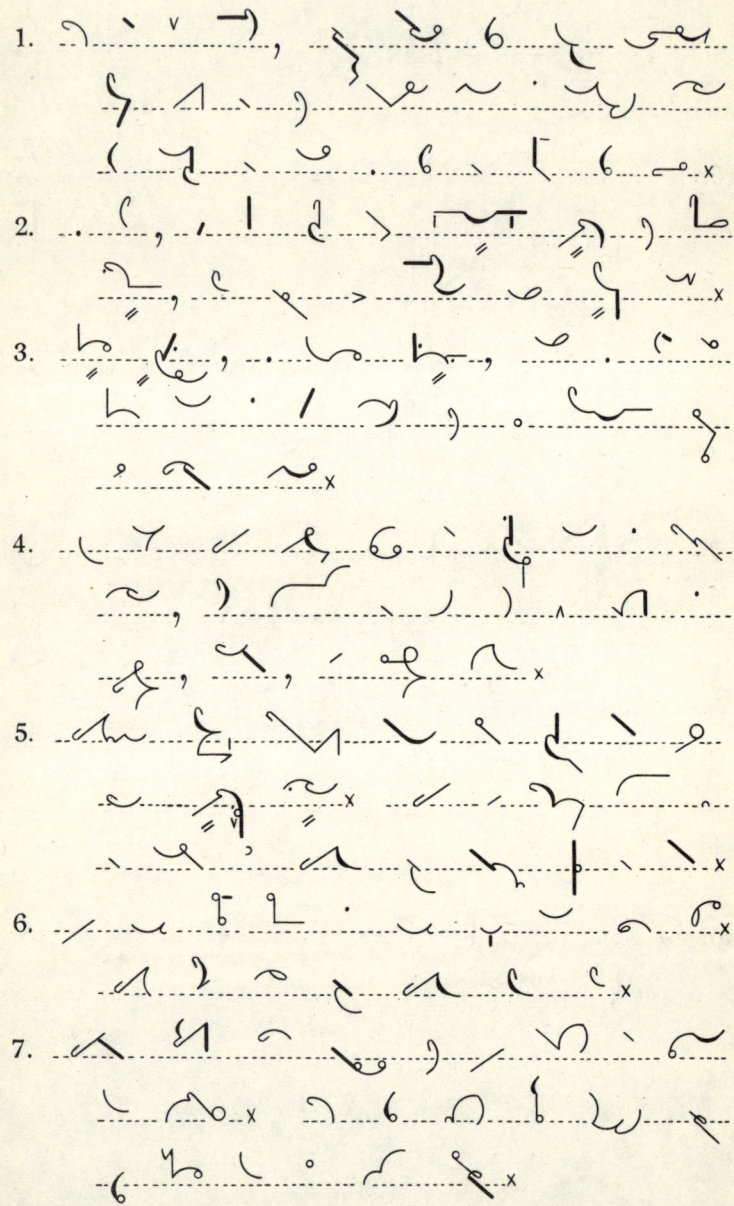

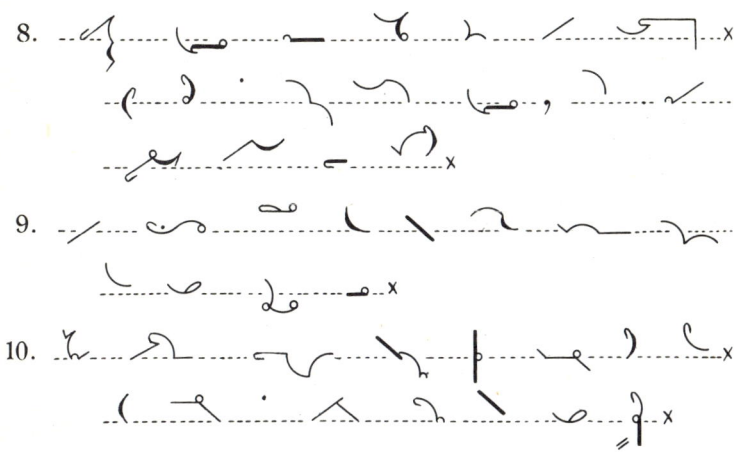

EXERCISE 82
(*Write in Shorthand*)

Frost Brothers, 120 Jefferson Avenue, Denver, Colorado.

Dear-Sirs: *We-are* afraid *that-it*-will-not-*be* possible *to*-recover-*the* total sum due *on-your* claim unless *you* adopt *different* measures. *We-have* used *special* efforts, *but* up *to-the* present *we-have* met *with* no success *in-our* endeavors *to-get-the* debtor *to* settle. *We-are*-unable-*to* collect *any* money, *nor can-we* extract *any* promise *from-him.*

We-think-you-will-*be*-obliged finall*y* to pass-*the* claim *over to-your* attorneys. Please notify us if-*you wish-us* to proceed *with-the* case *and* take *this* step *for-you*. *Very*-truly-*yours,* (100)

CHAPTER XII

46. N Hook

(*a*) A small final hook, written on the inside of curves, adds *n*:

fine, *phone*, *often*, *even*, *seven*, *than*, *then*, *zone*, *shown*, *machine*, *man*, *men*, *mean*, *remain*, *salesman*, *mine*, *nine*, *none*, *known*, *line*, *loan*, *iron*, *earn*, *women*

(*b*) The *n* hook is written on the non-circle side of all straight strokes:

pen, *pain*, *open*, *plan*, *brown*, *ten*, *ton*, *retain*, *gotten*, *forgotten*, *fifteen*, *bulletin*, *done*, *pardon*, *drawn*, *kitchen*, *join*, *June*, *imagine*, *clean*, *American*, *taken*, *gone*, *green*, *begin*, *rain*, *run*, *one*, *everyone*, *win*, *between*, *children*

Final *r*, when hooked, is usually written upward:

turn, *return*, *learn*, *western*, *corn*, *pattern*

SHORT FORMS

been, *general*, or *generally*, *within*, *southern*, *northern*, *opinion*

Phrases: *had been*, *have been*, *more than*, *better than*, *larger than*, *smaller than*, *our own*, *their own*

EXERCISE 83

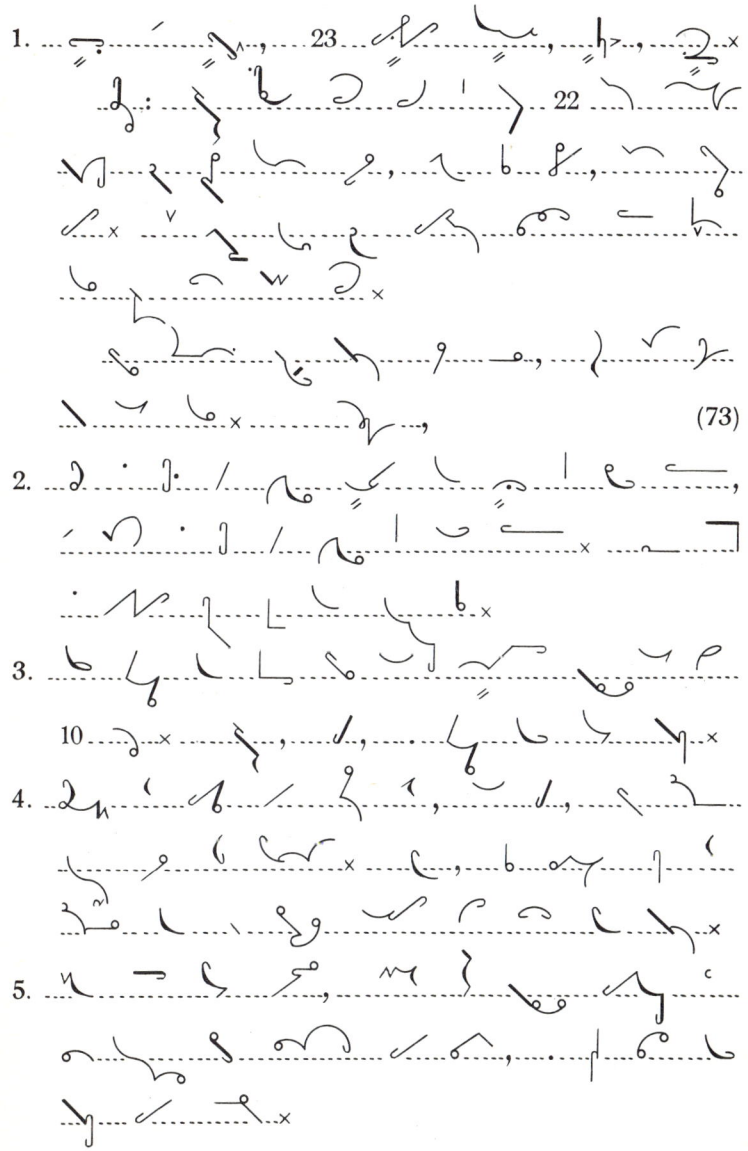

EXERCISE 84

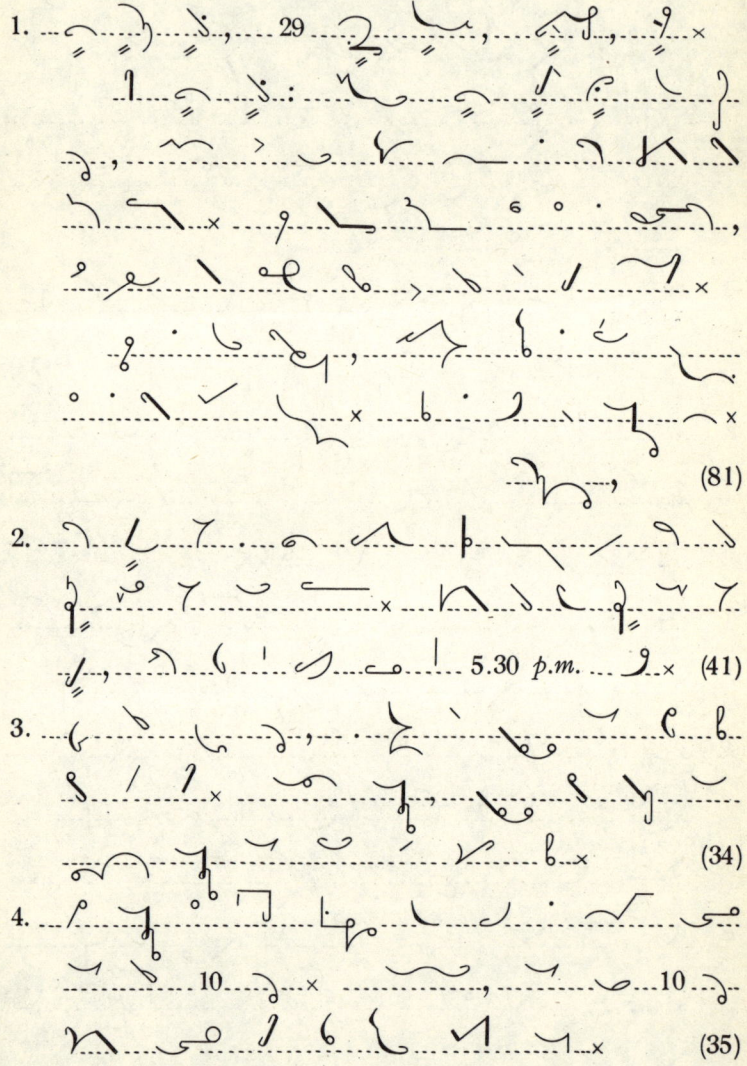

PITMAN SHORTHAND

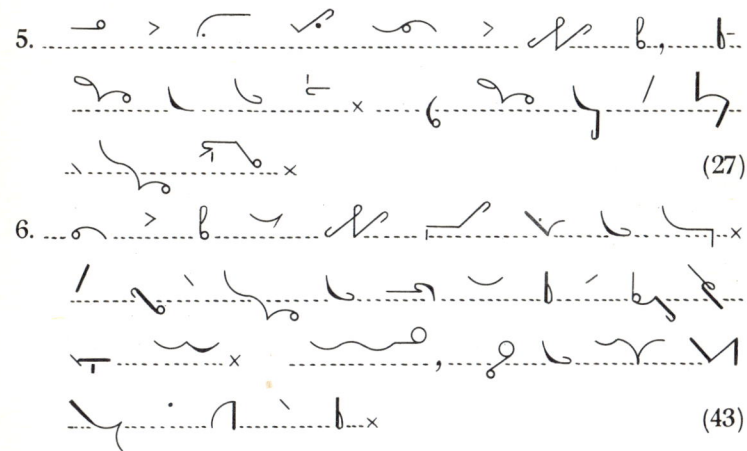

(27)

(43)

47. *F* or *V* Hook

A small final hook, written on the circle side of all straight strokes, adds *f* or *v*:

brief, *proof,* or *prove*, *approve*, *above*, *active*, *relative*, *attractive*, *drive*, *achieve*, *gave*, *rough*, *serve*, *deserve*, *preserve*, *reserve*, *wife*, *half*

There is no *f* or *v* hook to curves.

SHORT FORMS

represent, or *represented*   *representative*   *behalf*

advantage   Phrases: *out of*   *number of*

instead of   *which have*   *who have*

EXERCISE 85

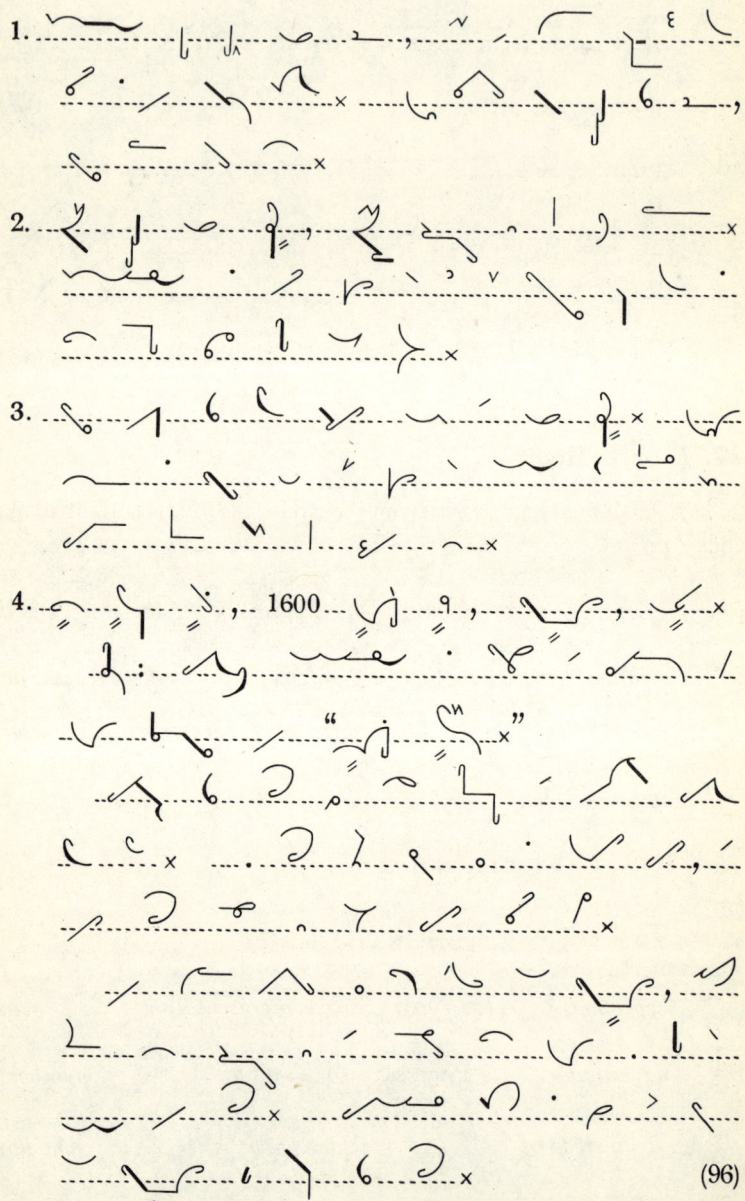

(96)

EXERCISE 86

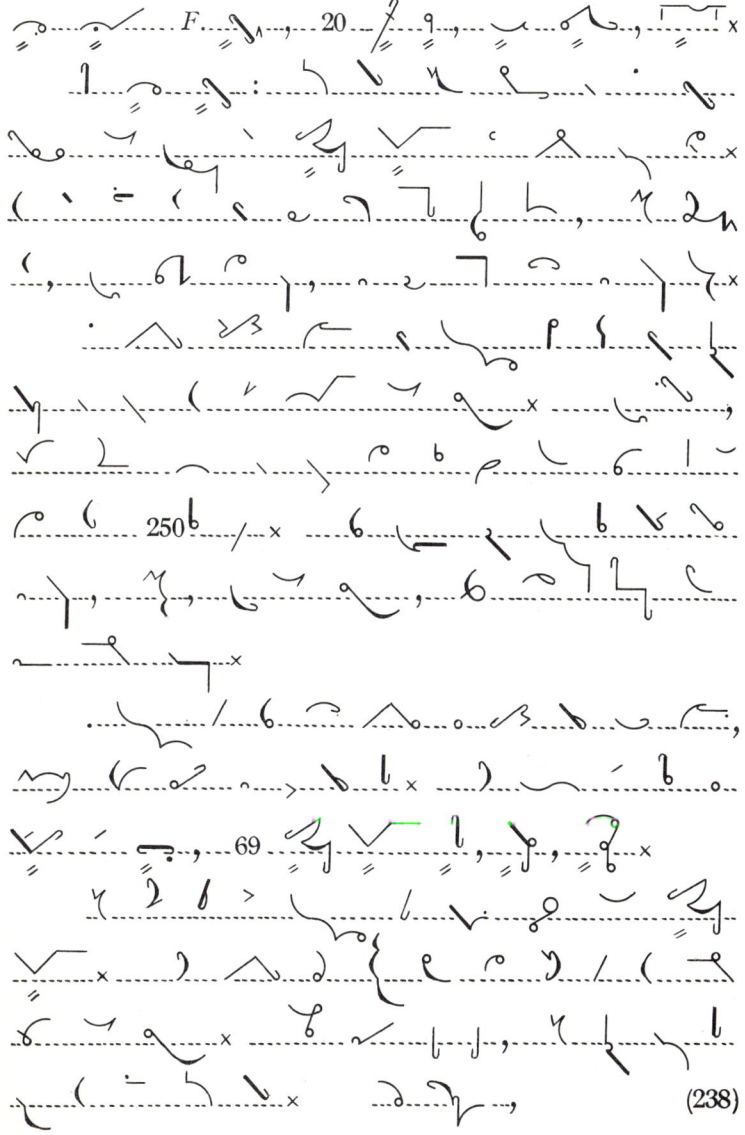

(238)

48. A finally hooked stroke is halved to indicate a following *t* or *d*:

(a) find, found, event, meant, or mend, demand, mind, amount, moment, statement, payment, movement, settlement, shipment, friend, front, department, land, around

(b) opened, band, print, plant, or planned, spent, or spend, point, pound, bound, attend, extent, or extend, instant, assistant, stand, president, kind, count, account, discount, second, grand, inclined, went, want, turned, current, round, returned

(c) approved, gift, served, draft, achieved, deserved, reserved, observed

SHORT FORMS

gentleman, gentlemen, cannot, told, tried, trade, toward, third

Phrases: had not, or do not, did not

If it is necessary to indicate in your shorthand notes that a longhand abbreviation is to be used, write a fully vocalized outline for the abbreviation:

hadn't, don't, didn't, doesn't, haven't, won't, isn't, couldn't, can't

NOTE: can not (separate words)

EXERCISE 87

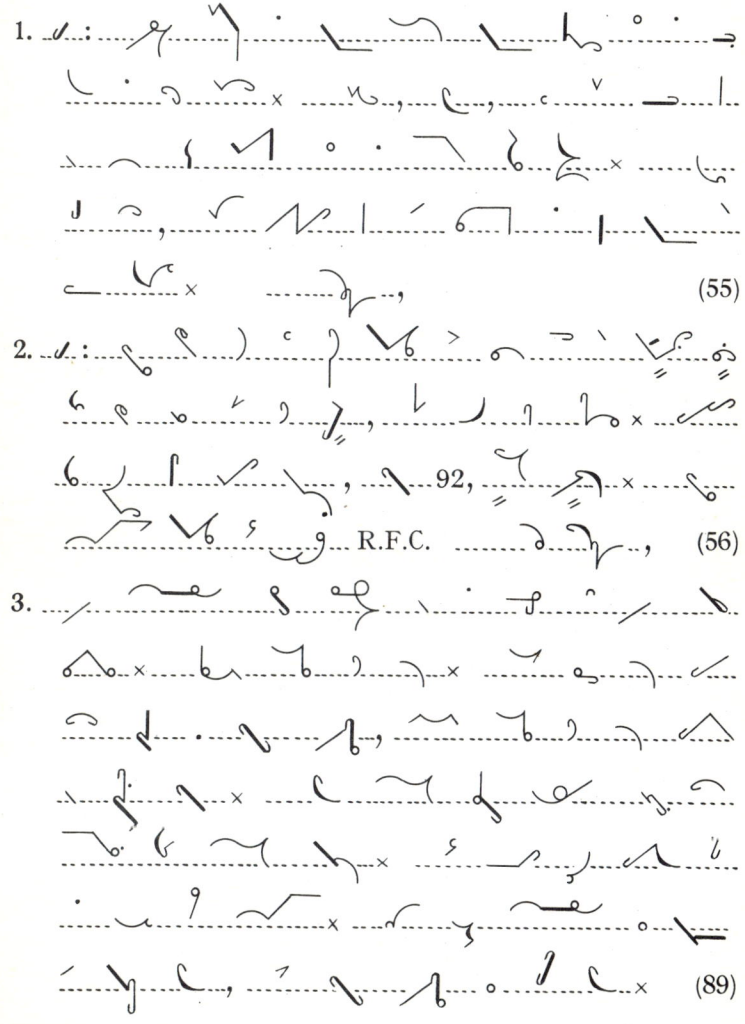

EXERCISE 88

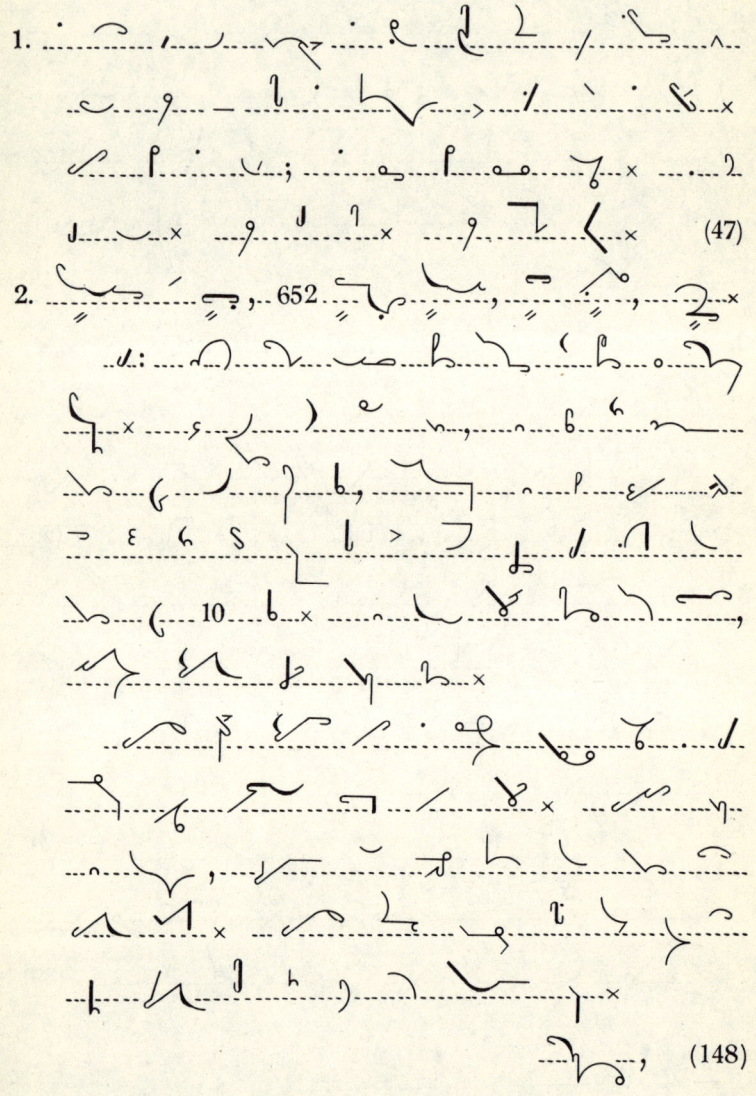

EXERCISE 89
(*Write in Shorthand*)

Bayne Brothers, 26 Lexington Avenue, Boston, Massachusetts.

Gentlemen: Please be kind-enough *to* supply-*the* items *on-the* attached list *as*-soon-*as*-possible. At-*the* present moment *there-is an* active demand *for-them, and-we*-hope *that-we-can* count *on hav*ing *them within* three days. *In-the* event *that-you-cannot* supply *them within that*-time, please-*inform*-us by return mail.

Please-note-*that-the* exact items specified *are to-be* supplied. If-*you-are* out-*of* stock *of any of-the* items, *do*-not supply *different* articles. Anything *that-is*-not exactly *as* specified must *be* returned.

We-enclose *our* check for $65 *which-is to-be* applied *toward our* account. *Yours*-truly, (112)

49. The final hooks are used in the middle of a word when they join easily to the following strokes:

(a) evening, finance, arrange, arrangement, opening, planning, training, attended, splendid, extended, merchandise, hundred, beginning

(b) perfect, profit, provide, provided, private, advance, definite, definitely, telephone, refer, prefer

(c) pointing, standing, spending, finding, printing, amounting, mountain, extending, apparently, memorandum, correspondence, country, kindly, kindness but note: *wanted*, *printed*, *meantime*, *seconded*, *accounted*

EXERCISE 90

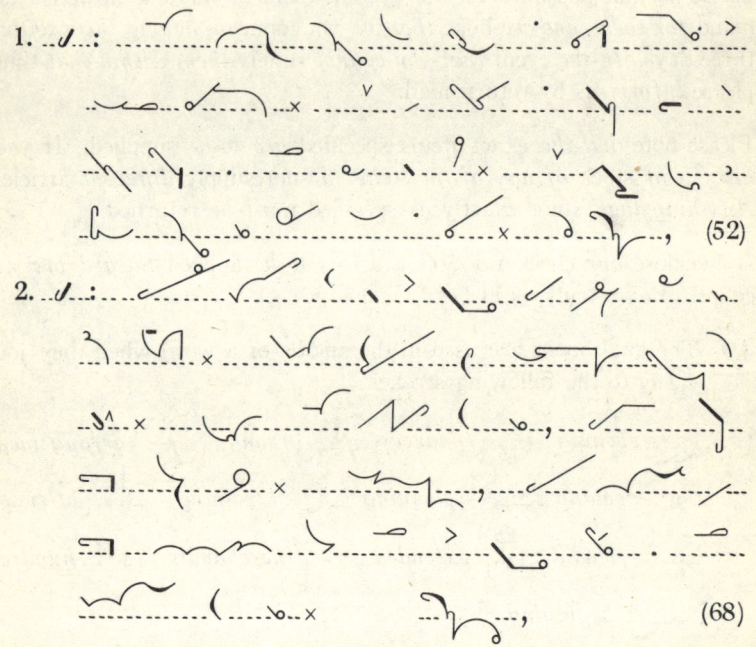

EXERCISE 91

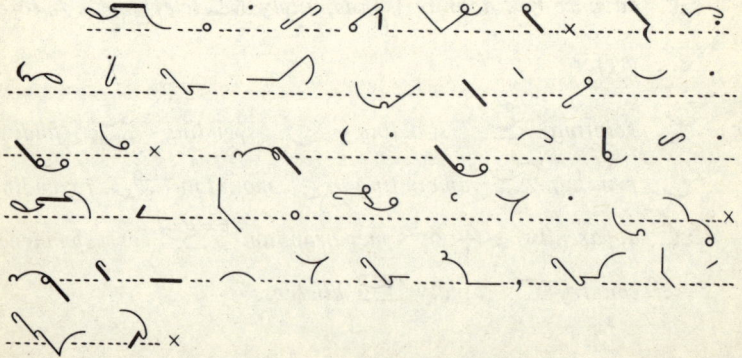

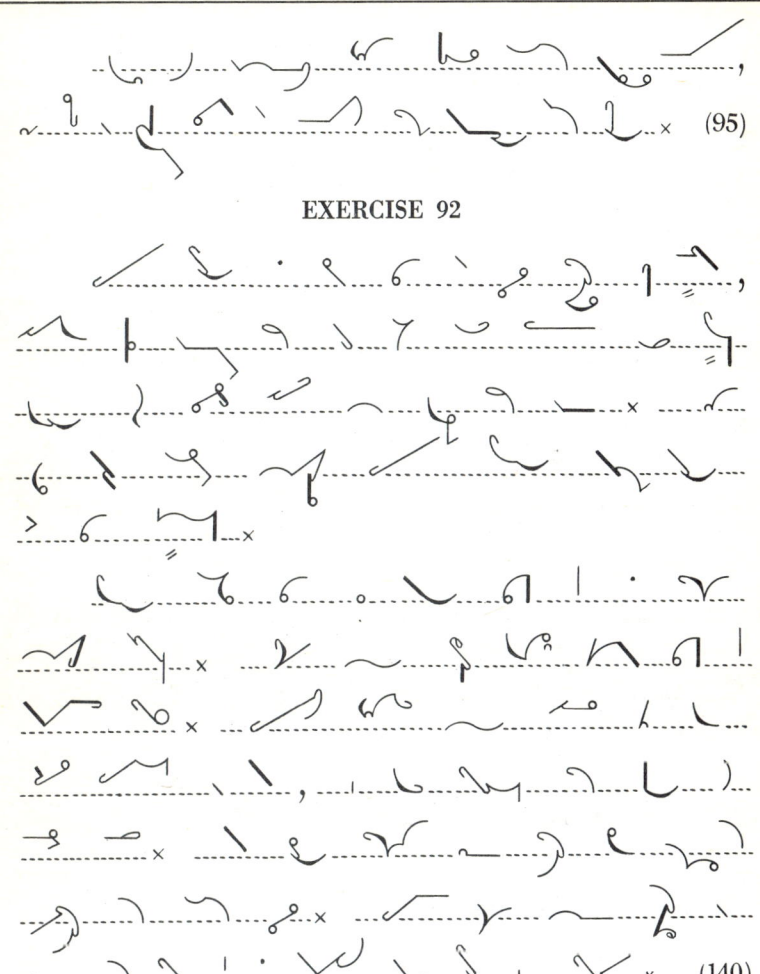

EXERCISE 92

(140)

50. Final *s* circle is written inside the *f* or *v* hook:

proofs, or proves   relatives   drafts   achieves

deserves   reserves   wives   gifts

representatives   advantages

51. A final circle, or a final loop, written on the same side of a straight stroke as the *n* hook, includes the *n:*

chance chances expense expenses distance
dance dances danced plans instance
instances turns returns once accounts
against bonds wants attends pounds
stands students depends reference references

52. The small circle is written inside the *n* hook attached to curves, and adds the final sound *z* only:

means remains loans funds friends
earns women's events demands

53. After a curved stroke the light sound *-nce* is represented by stroke *n* and the final *s* circle:

offence announce allowance romance
offences fenced announced announces
announcing allow allowances

54. When a vowel follows *f, v,* or *n,* at the end of a word, it is necessary to write the stroke in order to place the vowel sign:

coffee cough funny fun county count
penny pen review rough

SHORT FORMS

difficult difficulty balance balanced
responsible great guard gold

Phrase: at once

EXERCISE 93

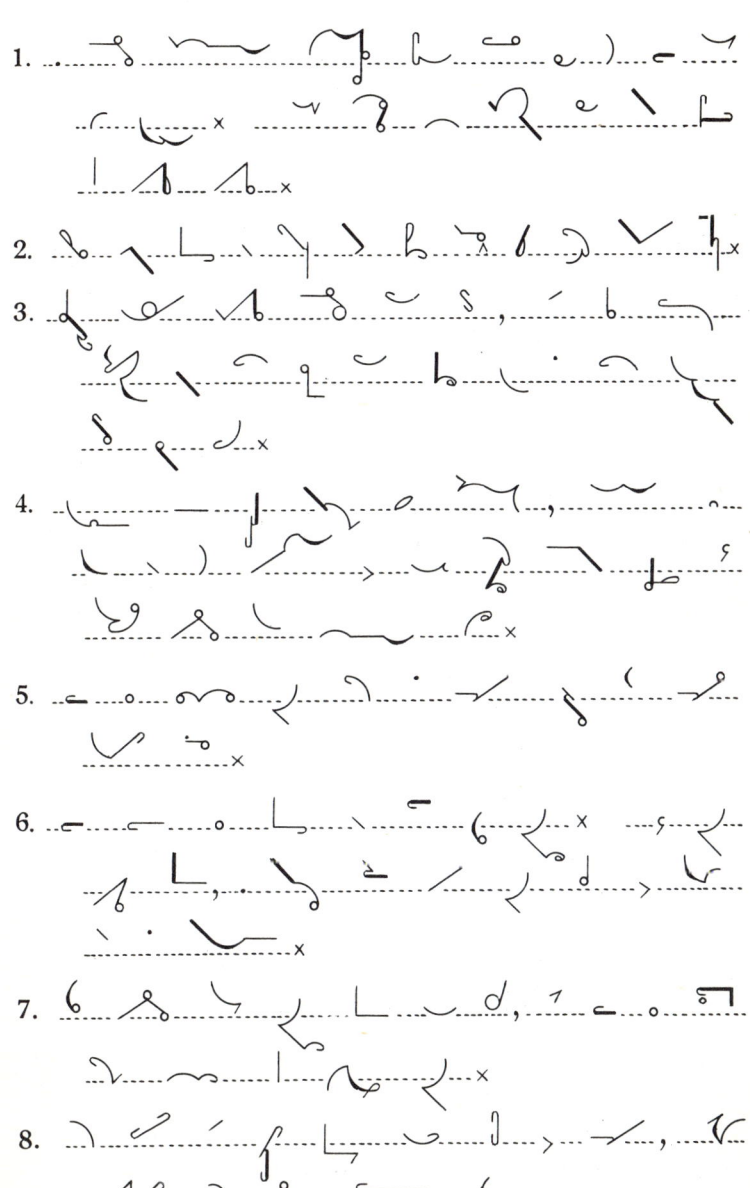

EXERCISE 94

PITMAN SHORTHAND

EXERCISE 95

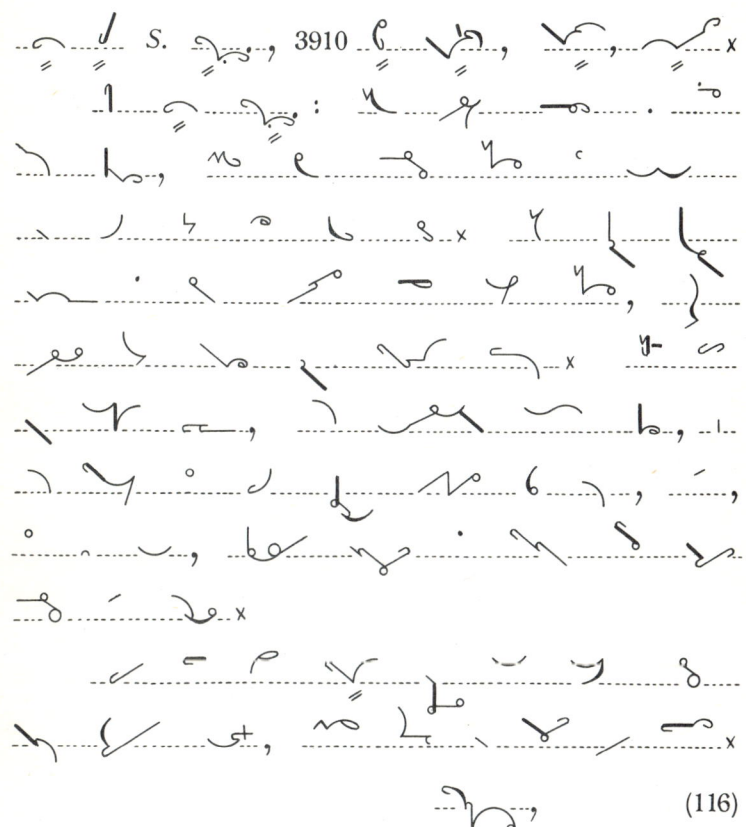

(116)

EXERCISE 96

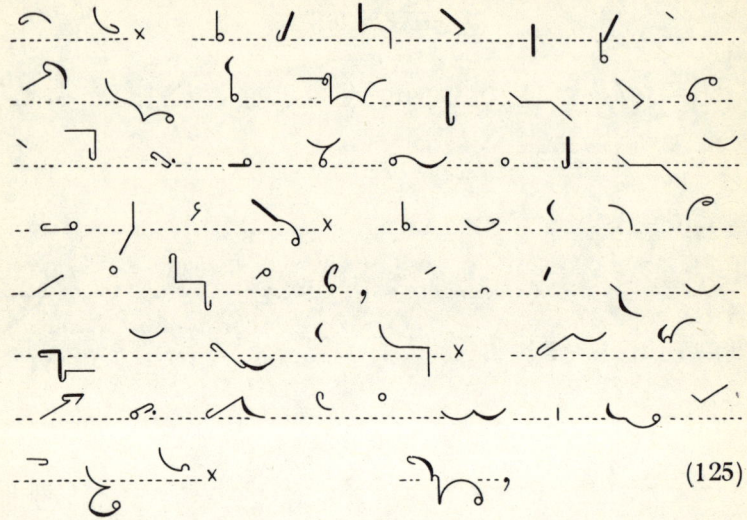

(125)

EXERCISE 97
(Write in Shorthand)

1. *This* firm furnished excellent references, so *we-think-we should* extend-*the* time *for*-payment *of-the balance* due *on-their*-account.

2. *The young*-man stands *a very*-good chance *of* obtaining-*the* post *of* assistant manager *of-the* bond department *owing to-the* splendid training he-*has* received.

3. Please provide us *with a* memorandum *of all* merchandise *which-is* subject *to a special* allowance.

4. *The* rough draft serves *to* show *how-the* use *of-the* telephone *has-been* extended *during-the* last seven *years*.

5. *Several of-the* students *have-been* taken out-*of-the* second grade, *and-we* plan *to*-make other arrangements *for-those-who* remain.

6. *Your* statement *is* returned *because-the* amount *of-the* discount *which-you have* deducted *is*-not correct.

EXERCISE 98
(Write in Shorthand)

Messrs. Evans *and* Groves, 46 West *Third* Street, Houston, Texas.

Gentlemen: We would-be ungrateful indeed if-*we*-did-not accept *your* kind hint. *As a* direct result *we-have* planned *a* series *of* trips *for our representatives which-will* bring *them in*to closer touch *with our* customers *all-over-the* United-States. *Our* men leave New-York at-once *with* samples *of-our* advance lines. They-will explain *to-you-the* reasons *for-the* apparent slackness *we-have* shown *during-the* past season. *It-has-been* one *of-much* stress *for*-us, *and-we-are*-inclined-*to-think* you-will make-*the* proper allowances *when-you* learn-*the* reason.

You-will-*be*-glad *to* know *that-the* new lines *to-be* shown *to-you have-been* favorably received *in-the northern* states. They-*are of* splendid value, *and are* sold at-prices *that give*-us *a very*-low margin *of*-profit. *Yours very*-truly, (144)

CHAPTER XIII

55. -*Shun* Hook

A large final hook adds the final syllable -*shun*. This large hook is written on the inside of curves:

fashion   *motion*   *nation*   *relation*   *attention*
examination   *session*   *division*   *explanation*
extension   *profession*   *supervision*   *mention*
admission   *expansion*   *intention*

The *s* circle is added as shown: *fashions*   *nations*   *relations*

When a good joining is obtained, the large hook is used when the -*shun* syllable occurs in the middle of a word:

national   *professional*   *intentional*

EXERCISE 99

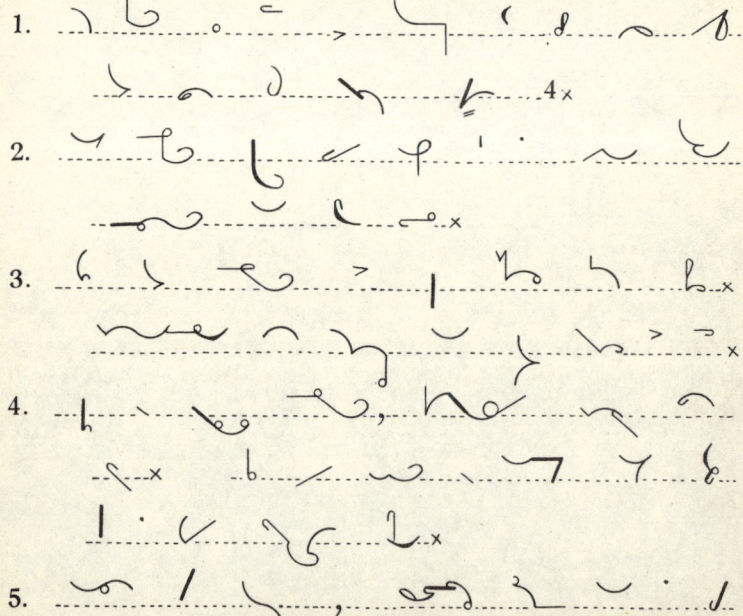

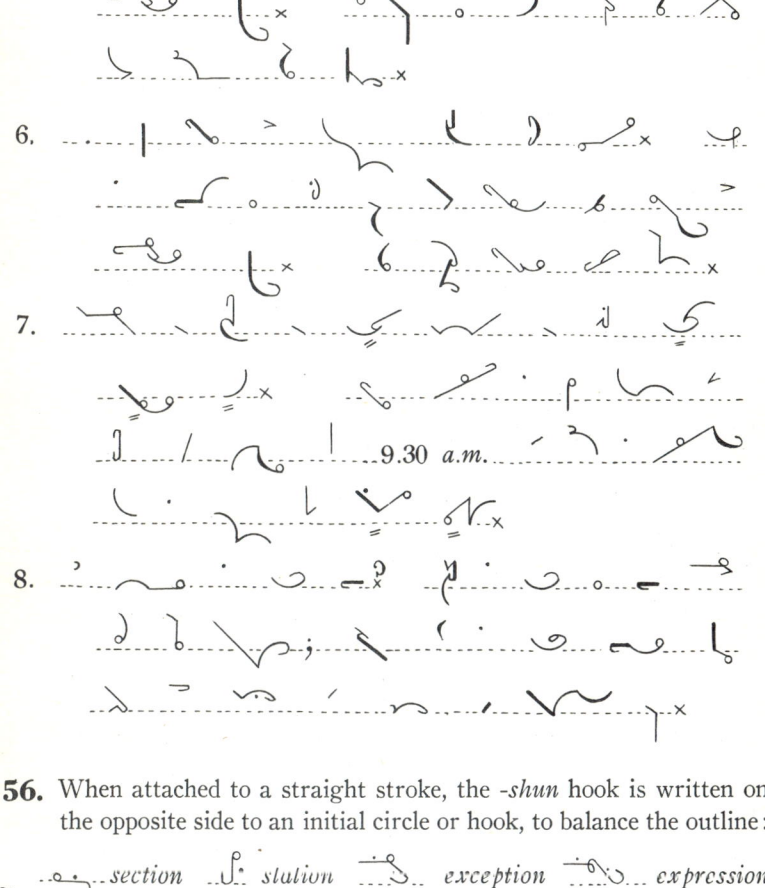

56. When attached to a straight stroke, the *-shun* hook is written on the opposite side to an initial circle or hook, to balance the outline:

⌒ section ⌒ station ⌒ exception ⌒ expression
⌒ transaction ⌒ reception ⌒ anticipation ⌒ discussion
⌒ recollection ⌒ registration ⌒ exceptionally

After ⌒ ⌒ and ⌒ the *-shun* hook is written away from the curve, to balance the outline:

⌒ fiction ⌒ vacation ⌒ vocation ⌒ location ⌒ selection
⌒ vocational ⌒ affectionate

EXERCISE 100

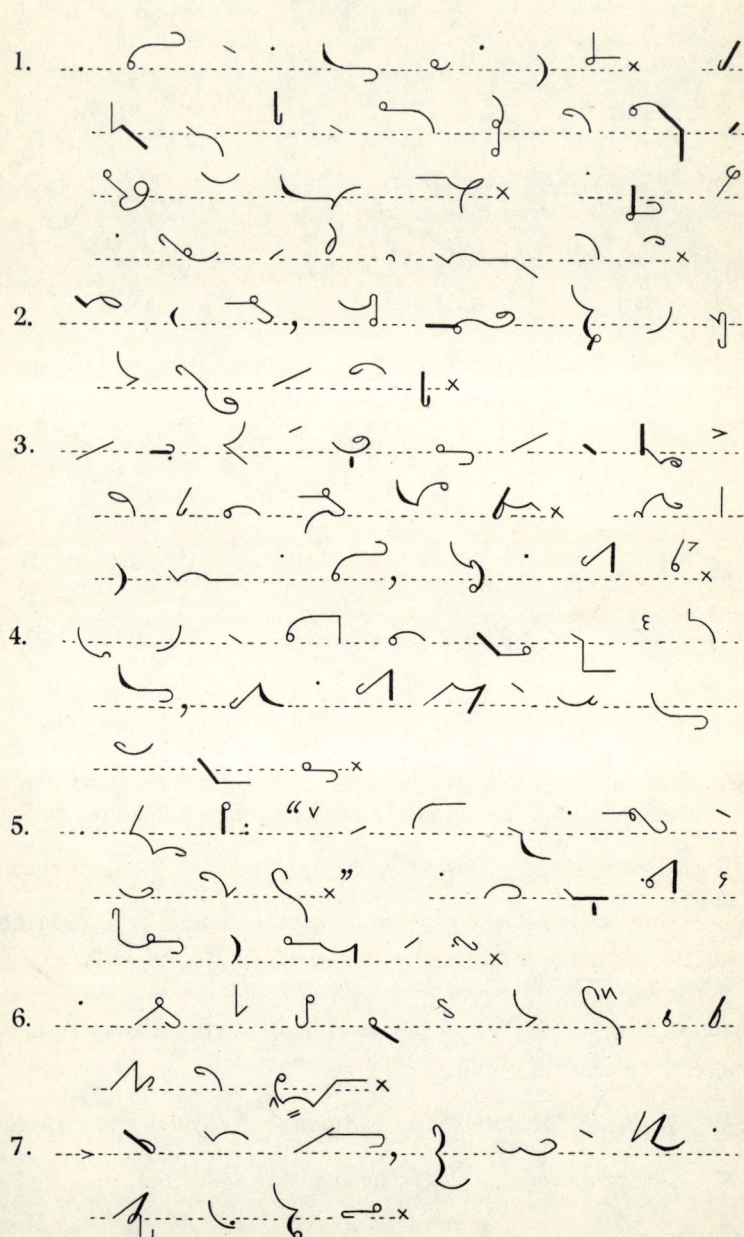

PITMAN SHORTHAND

8.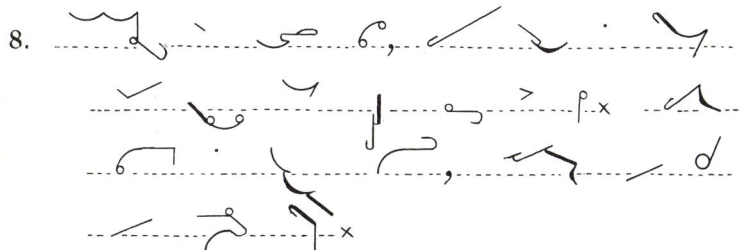

57. The *-shun* hook is written on the right side of simple *t, d,* or *j*:

notation   invitation   expectation   imitation

presentation   reputation   petition   addition

edition   additional   magician

When added to other simple straight strokes, *-shun* is written on the side opposite to the last vowel:

action   caution   portion   operation   occasion

education   application   distribution   election

direction   attraction   deduction   obligation

reduction   occupation   educational   occasional

occasionally

EXERCISE 101

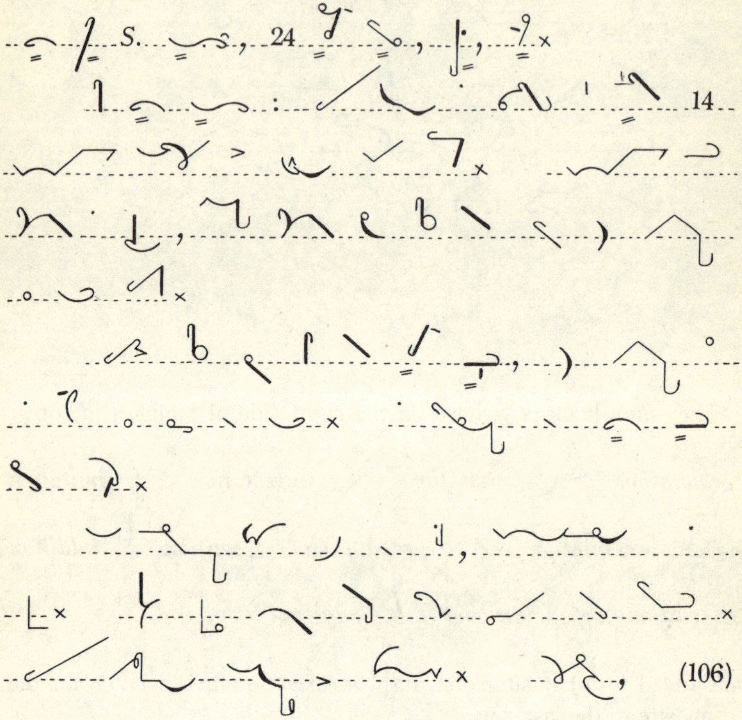

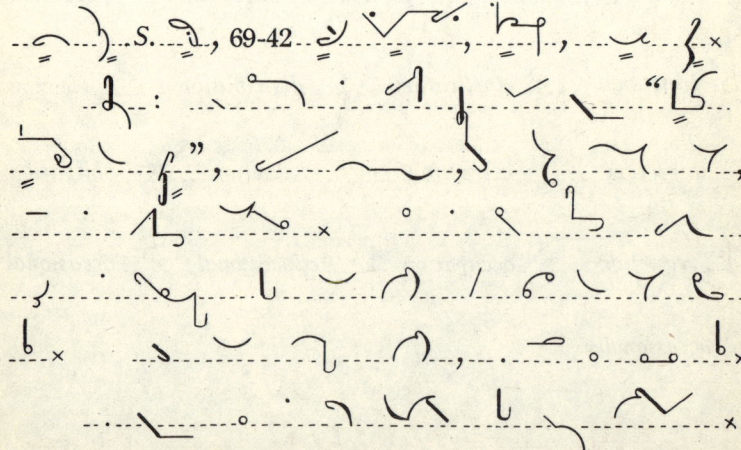

EXERCISE 102

(120)

58. S-Shun

When -*shun* follows the *s* circle or the *ns* circle, it is represented by a small curl (a continuation of the circle). A third-place vowel between the *s* and -*shun* is placed outside the curl. Any other vowel is not indicated.

decision   *position*   *opposition*   *disposition*

proposition   *possession*   *taxation*   *physician*

musician   *succession*   *sensation*   *transition*

A final *s* circle is placed inside the curl:

possessions   *decisions*   *physicians*   *transitions*

59. In words ending in -*uation* or -*uition*, the stroke *sh* and *n* hook are generally used:

situation   *tuition*

A stroke hooked for -*shun* is halved to indicate a final *t* or *d*:

motioned   *cautioned*   *fashioned*

SHORT FORMS

information   *public, publish,* or *published*   *publication*
object, or *objected*   *objection*   *organize,* or *organized*
organization   *satisfaction*   *investigation*   *yesterday*

EXERCISE 103

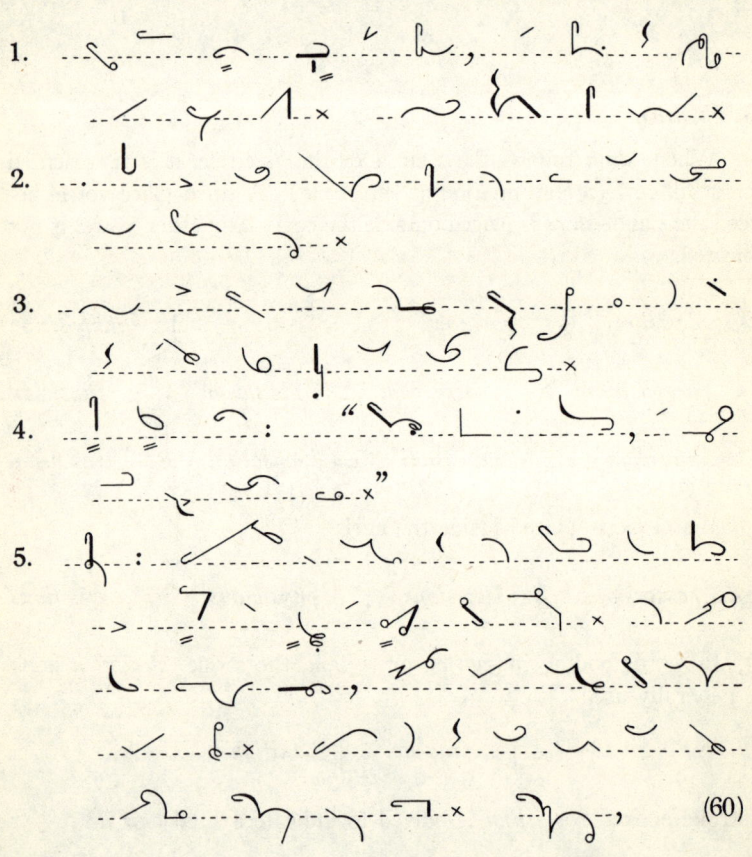

(60)

EXERCISE 104

(145)

EXERCISE 105

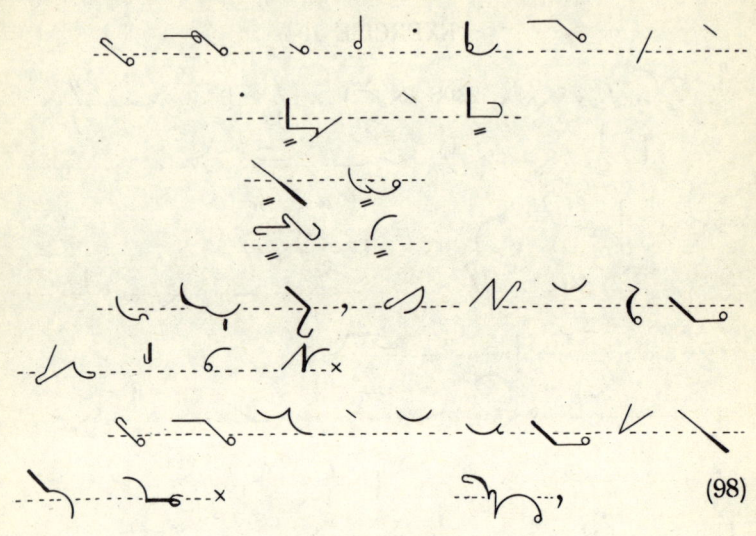

(98)

EXERCISE 106

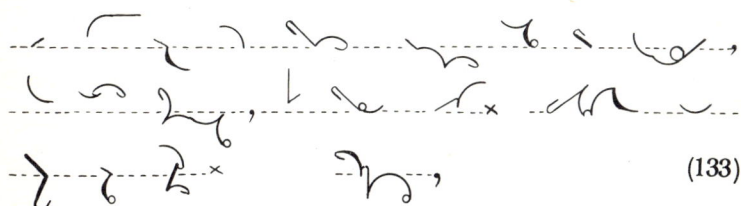

(133)

EXERCISE 107
(*Write in Shorthand*)

Muir *and* Richman, 6 College Street, New Haven, Connecticut. Attention *of* Mr. Frank Smith.

Gentlemen: We-think-we-are in a position *to* assist *you to-tell in what* direction *your* promotion work may best *be* extended. *As you-are*-no-doubt aware, *our organization has-given* many *years of* attention *to*-problems *of* distribution *of*-every *description, and-the information in-our*-possession *is* nation wide *and* reliable.

We-believe-that-you would-find *a* discussion *of-the* problem *with our* Mr. Jones *of*-value *to-you*. He-will-*be*-glad *to*-receive *an* invitation *from-you to-call. Very*-truly-*yours,* (89)

EXERCISE 108
(*Write in Shorthand*)

Mr. James Merrigan, 42 St. Marks Place, Brooklyn, *New York*.

Dear-Sir: *With-the* small amount *of information in-our*-possession, *we-are*-unable-*to give-you a* definite decision *on-your* application *for a* loan. *You*-make no mention *at-all of any* provision *for* expansion at-*your* present location, *nor do you tell*-us if-*you have any* intention *of*-taking *over-the* operation *of more* machines.

However, we-believe-that-the proposition *is* certainly worth discussion, *but, of*-course, action must wait *till-you* furnish us *with* additional *information* about *your* plans.

We-suggest *that-you call* at-*our* office sometime *during-the-next* few days, *to*-permit us *to-go over* every angle *of-the* situation *with-you*. *Yours*-truly, (114)

CHAPTER XIV

60. Compound Consonants

Besides the double consonants in the *pel* and *per* series, there are six compound consonants:

Letter	Sign	Name	As in
KW		kwa	quick, request
GW		gwa	guava, linguist
MP, MB		emp / emb	camp, embody
LR		ler	filler, scholar
RR		rer	poorer, sharer
WH		hwa	where, whip

1. quickly, quit, quote, quoted, quoting, quarter, quantity, acquaintance, acquainted, equipment, banquet, inquiry, request, requested, require, requirements, square, exquisite, adequate, Maguire, linguist

2. camp, campaign, stamp, dump, lump, sympathy, embody, impose, imposes, imposition

PITMAN SHORTHAND

3. roller counsellor ruler scholars
4. bearer fairer admirer poorer sharer wearer
5. where white somewhere anywhere nowhere everywhere elsewhere

When *m* is immediately followed by *pr, br, pl,* or *bl*, the double consonant strokes are used:

impress embrace imply emblem

Ler is used only where the downward *l* would be used; *rer* is used only where the downward *r* would be used.

SHORT FORMS

whether important, or importance improve, improved, or improvement impossible accord, according, or according to cared particular opportunity

EXERCISE 109

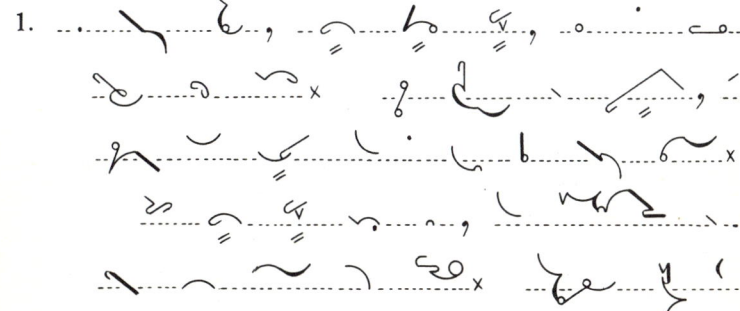

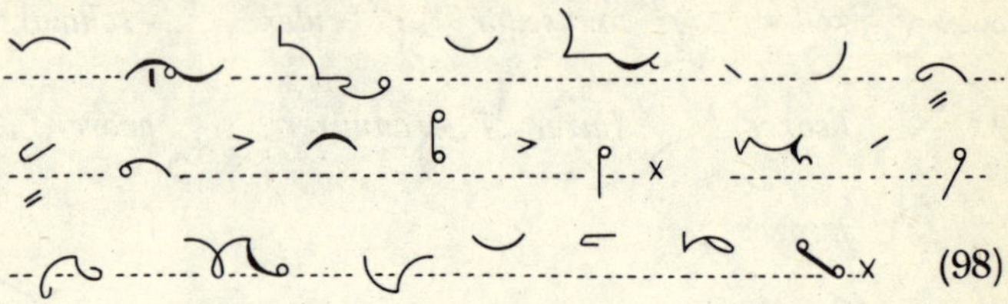

(98)

2. (69)

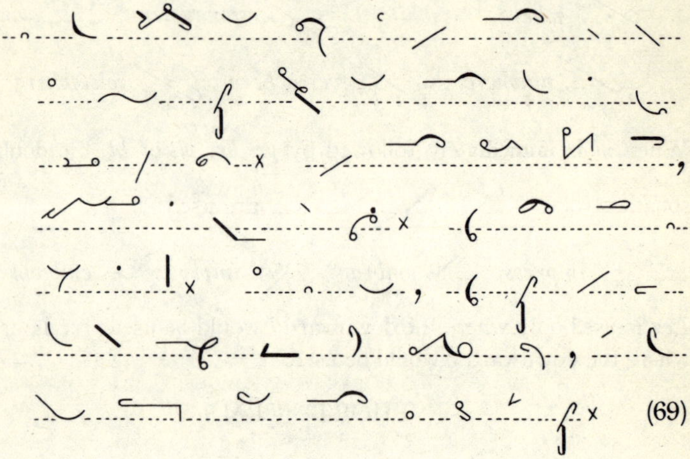

EXERCISE 110

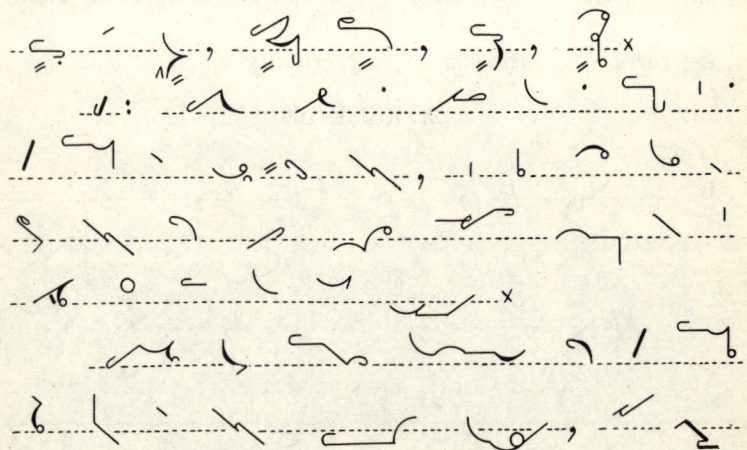

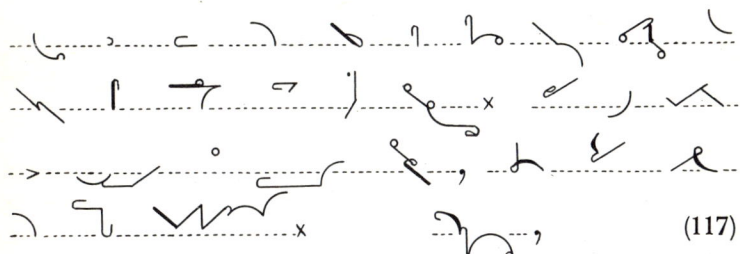

(117)

EXERCISE 111

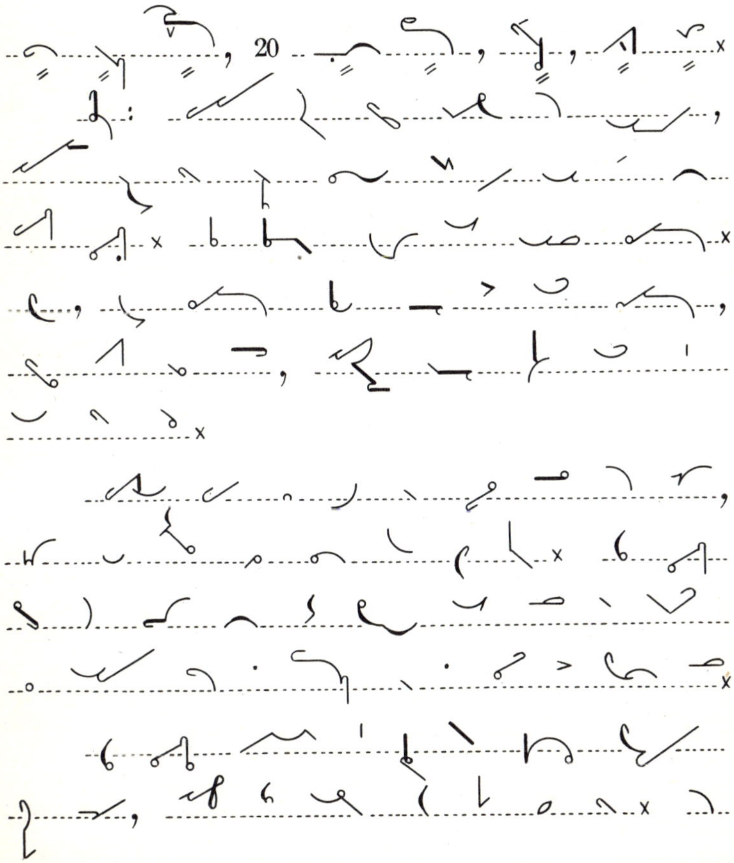

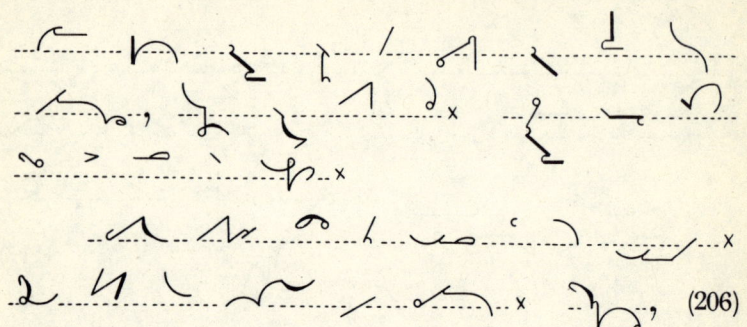

61. *Wl* and *Whl*

A small initial hook prefixes *w* to upward *l*. A large initial hook prefixes *wh* to upward *l*. These hooks are read first:

well   will   willing   unwilling   wild   wall   wealth   Walton

while   wheel   meanwhile

EXERCISE 112

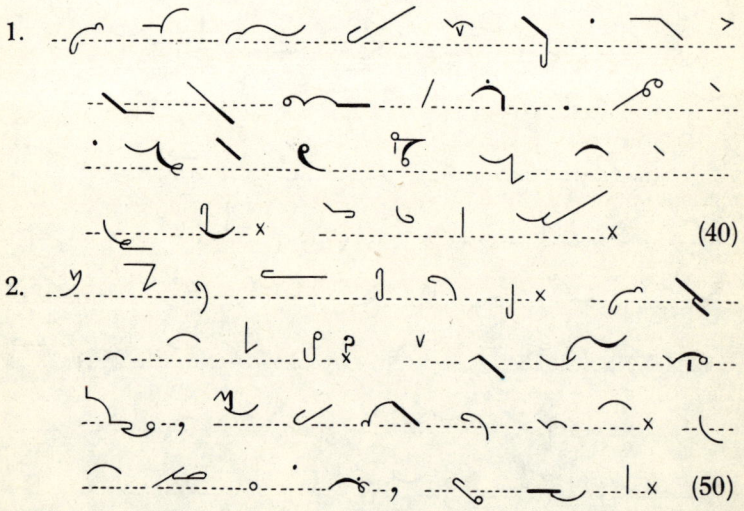

PITMAN SHORTHAND 127

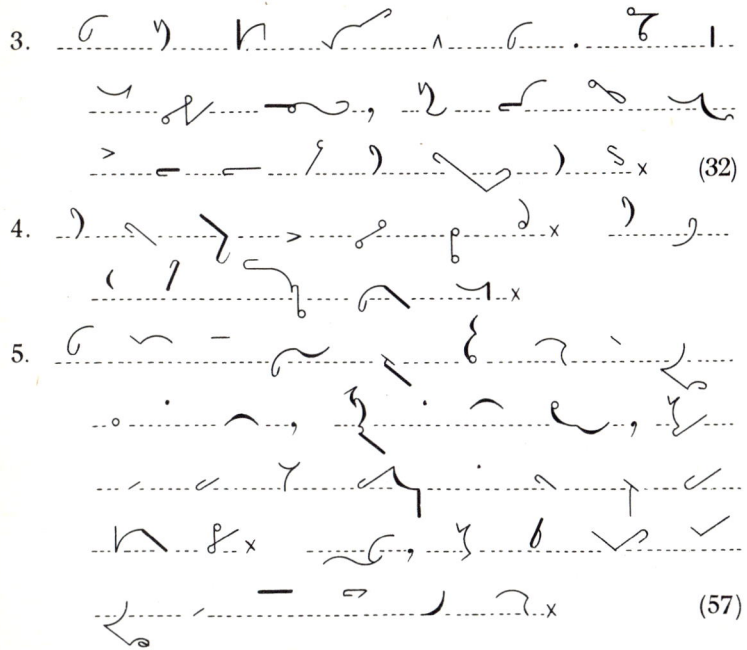

62. Tick and Dot *H*

Generally the upward form of *h* is used when this stroke is joined to other consonants. When *h* is the only consonant, or when it is followed by *k* or *g*, the downward form is used:

he   hug   hog   hook   Hague

(*a*) The upward form is used for half-length *h* standing alone.

hate   hot   hat   heat   height

(*b*) A small tick, written as shown, represents *h* before *m*, *l*, and downward *r*:

home   whom   Hamilton   hall   health   hello

help   hold   holiday   hair   hear, or here

her   herself   horse   hurt   harm

(c) Where it would be awkward to write the stroke *h* in the middle of a word, *h* is represented by a light dot placed alongside the vowel sound, as shown:

perhaps   neighborhood   likelihood   household

Manhattan

EXERCISE 113

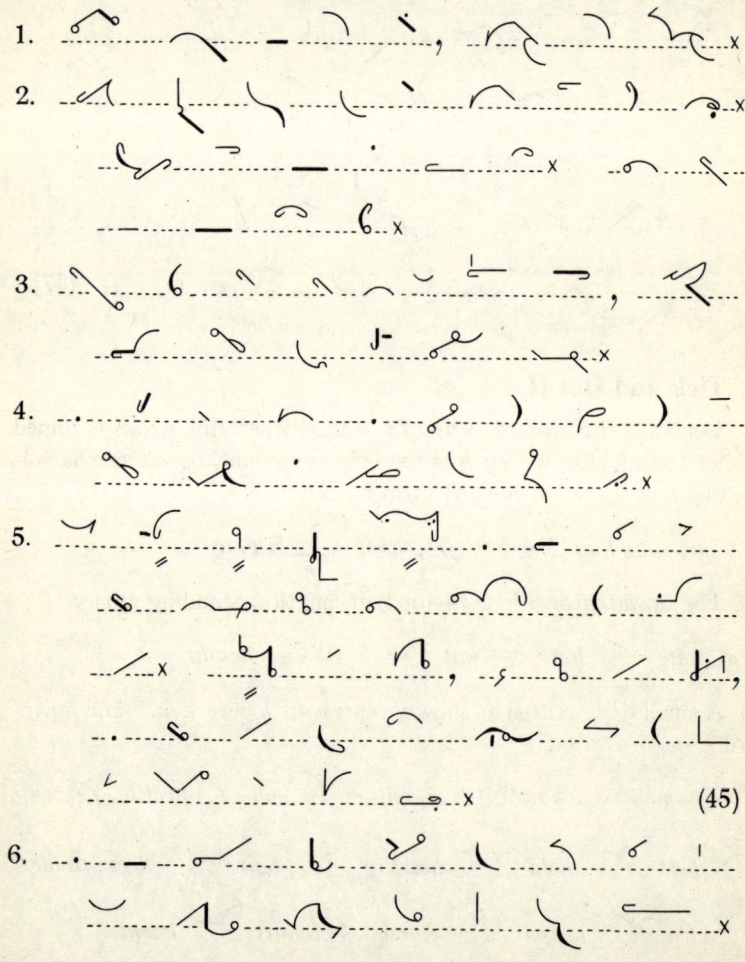

PITMAN SHORTHAND

(75)

63. Contractions

Where a consonant is only lightly sounded in certain cases it is omitted:

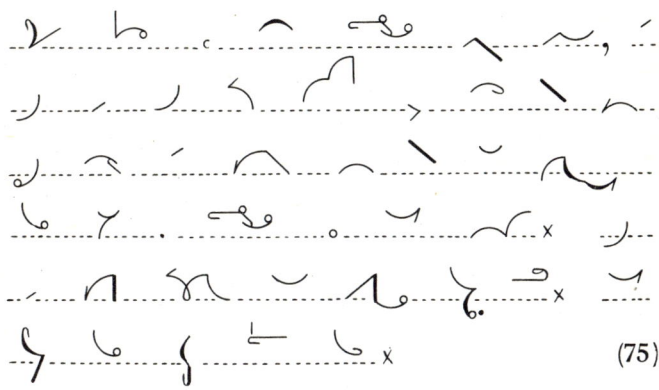

EXERCISE 114

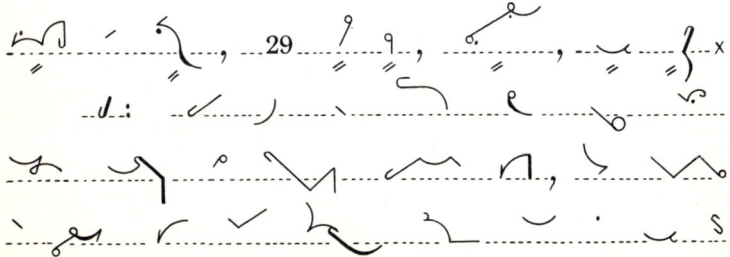

EXERCISE 115

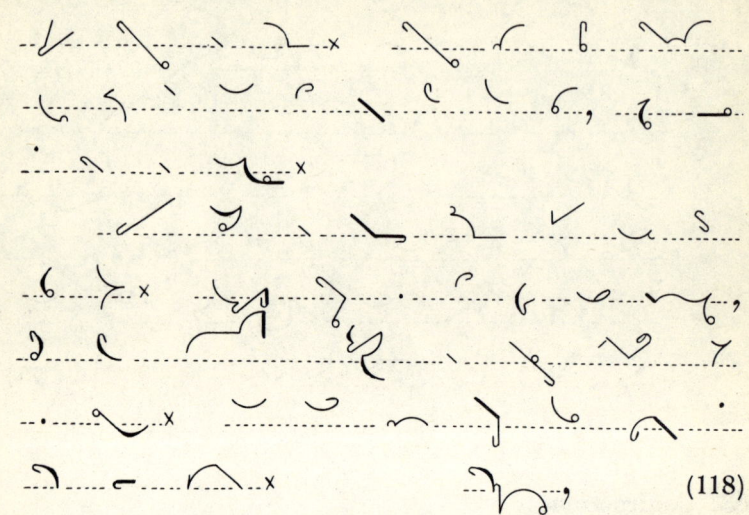

(118)

(135)

EXERCISE 116

(*Write in Shorthand*)

1. Henry R. Waters &-Sons, 642 Harrison Avenue, Cleveland, Ohio.

Gentlemen: We-are anxious *to*-receive-*the* package *of* pens *which according-to your* invoice *of November* 14 *was sent* by-mail five days ago. *We*-presume *that-the* package *was sent* by registered mail.

In-answer *to-our* inquiry, *the* post-office here says *that-the* package *has*-not-yet-*been* received. *Do-you* think *that-there-has-been* a mistake *in* addressing-*the* package? *Yours very*-truly, (69)

2. Hamilton & Hickey, 20 Grand Street, Rochester, New-York.

Gentlemen: We-are-sorry *to*-learn *that-the* package *we-sent to-you* by registered mail *on* November 14 *has-not-been* received. Promptly upon receipt *of-your* note *we-sent a* duplicate package.

It-is-possible, *of*-course, *that-the* package *was* incorrectly addressed, *but-we-do*-not-*think that-there-is any* likelihood *that-this-is-the* case. *We-are* asking-*the* postal authorities *to* institute *a* search *for-the* lost package, *and*-no-doubt they-will-*be*-able-*to* find *it*.

Meanwhile, if-*the* original package *is delivered to-you,* will-*you*-kindly return *it to*-us. *The* cost *of* postage will-*be-sent to-you,* or *you-can* make *an* adjustment *in-your*-account *when-you* mail *your* check. *Very*-truly-*yours,* (126)

CHAPTER XV

64. Halving

There are a few additional applications of the halving principle. (*a*) The strokes *m* and *n* are halved and thickened to indicate a following *d:*

made mad madam moderate modern

middle seemed named ashamed assumed

end send signed sound intend thousand

designed telephoned indicate undoubtedly

need

(*b*) Downward *l* and downward *r* are halved and thickened to indicate a following *d:*

billed mailed child field old world

filed detailed yield failed installed

board appeared afford desired acquired

card insured assured heard wired

standard ordinary

EXERCISE 117

65. Final *lt* is expressed by ⌒ , and final *rt* is generally expressed by ⌒ :

belt   felt   built   fault   bolts   start   support   smart   sort   skirt   part   port   sport   report   export   import

66. When a vowel comes between *l-d* or *r-d,* the full strokes must be written:

carried   delayed   followed   married   valued   borrowed   worried

67. As indicated in paragraph 35b, strokes of unequal length must not be joined if their length would not clearly show. To show the difference in length, disjoin half length *t* or *d* following stroke *t* or *d*:

attitude   credited   treated   dictated   straightened   illustrated   postdated

Special use of disjoining: promptness   indebtedness   outfit

SHORT FORMS

short   hand   under   yard   word   immediate   school   schooled   spirit   certificate   knowledge   acknowledge

The halving principle is used to form the phrases   if it   if it is   in which it is   I am not   you are not   you will not   you were not   this would be

PITMAN SHORTHAND

EXERCISE 118

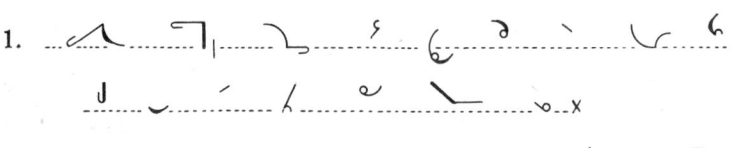

EXERCISE 119

1. 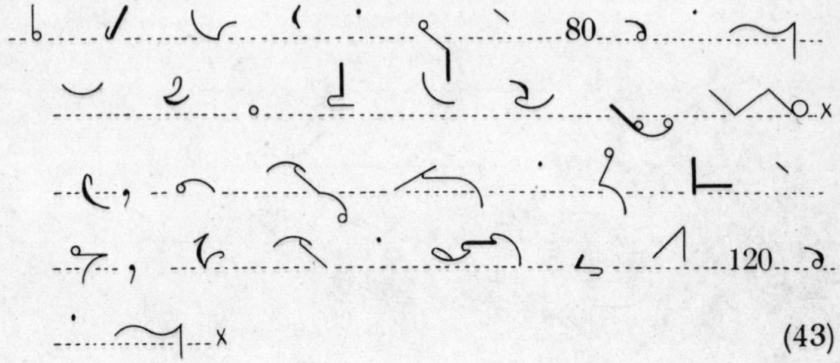 [shorthand] (43)

2. 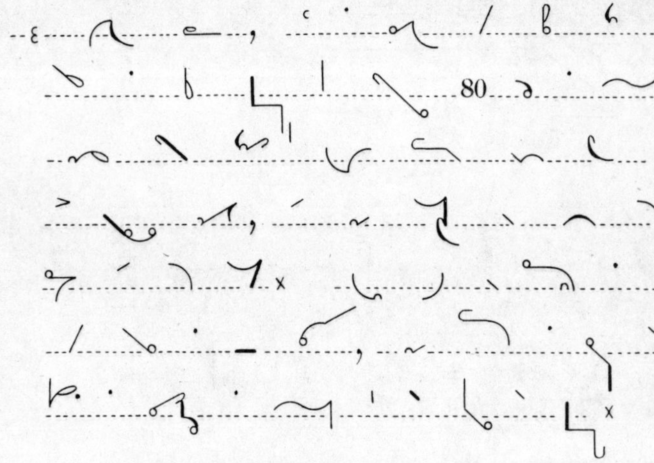 [shorthand] (80)

EXERCISE 120

1. 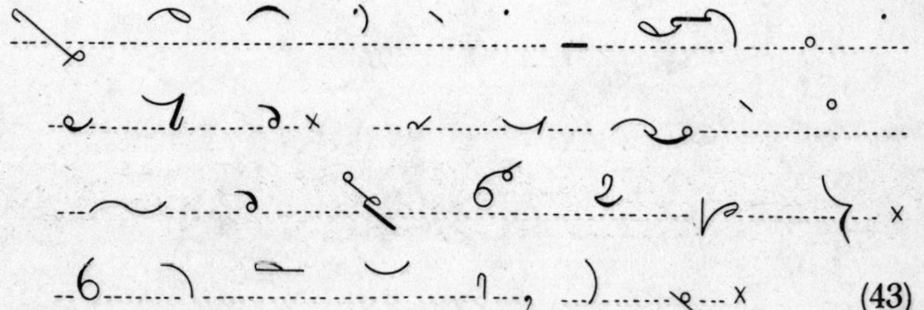 [shorthand] (43)

2. 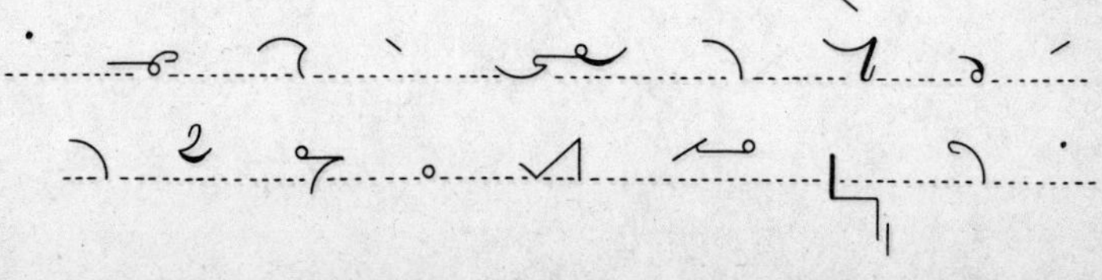 [shorthand]

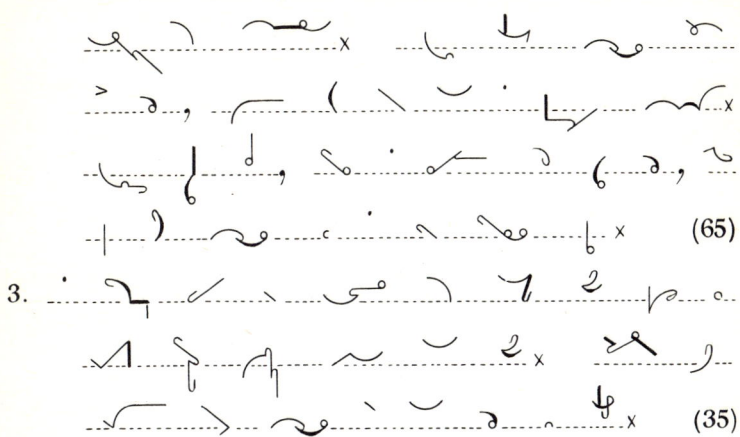

(65)

3. (35)

EXERCISE 121

(110)

EXERCISE 122

(Write in Shorthand)

Smart *and* Walsh, 62 *School* Street, Portland, Oregon.

Gentlemen: Please-*inform*-us *immediate*ly *when-we-*may *expect-the* lighting fixtures *we* ordered *from-you* on October *7, for-the* apartment house *we-are-*now *building. According-to* our *under*standing at *that-*time, *you-*were *to-deliver* them *towards-the* end *of-the-*month, *but-you* have failed *to do-*so.

It-is distinctly *under*stood, *of-*course, *that-the* delay *is-*not intentional *on-your* part, *but-we-have* received no *word from-you.* Please-*do-*not hesitate *to inform-*us *if-you-are-*not able-*to-*make *immediate delivery.* *We-think-you-*will-not mis*under*stand *our* attitude *when-we* say *that* *if-you-cannot deliver-them immediate*ly *we-shall-have to-*get *them* else-where. Work *is-*now *be*ing delayed, *and-we* simply *cannot* afford *to* wait. *Very-*truly-*yours,* (131)

68. Doubling Principle

Curved strokes are doubled in length to indicate a following syllable *tr, dr,* or *THr:*

after   father   afternoon   order   enter

motor   matter   mother   another   neither

center   central   sister   entertain   interview

elevator   Easter   federal   folder   holder

remainder   calendar   further   shorter   matters

orders

Stroke *l* standing alone, or with only a final *s* circle, is doubled to add *tr* only:

letter   letters   later   latter   alter, but

leader   older   leather

EXERCISE 123

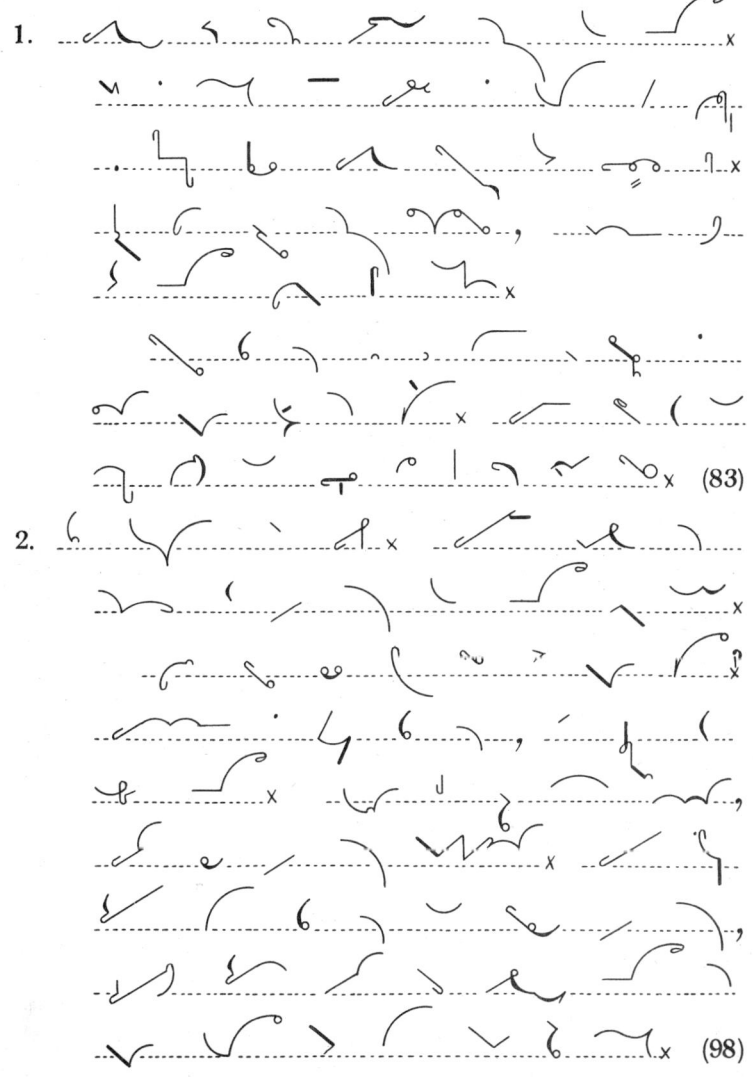

EXERCISE 124

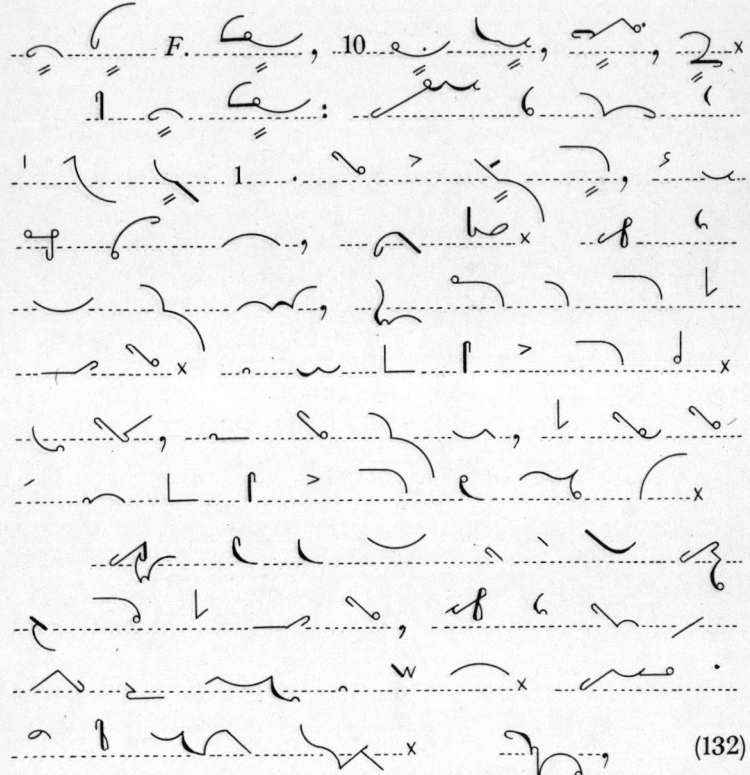

(132)

69. A straight stroke is doubled to indicate *tr, dr,* or *THr,* only
(1) when it follows another stroke or circle *s,* or
(2) when it has a finally joined diphthong or a final hook:

chapter   director   operator   educator
refrigerator   typewriter   scatter   powder
render   painter   tender   winter   wonder
renders   wonders, but   better   gather   weather
readers   platter   trader

70. In a few common words the syllable *-ture* is represented by the doubling principle:

future   *nature*   *natural*   *picture*

pictures   *signature*

71. The doubling principle is not used in past tenses:

rendered   *ordered*   *entered*   *centered*

72. *mp, mb,* is doubled to add final *-er:*

temper   *December*   *September*   *chamber*

ng is doubled to add final *kr* or *gr:*

Yonkers   *longer*   *hunger*

These double length forms are written when they are more convenient than the hooked forms { mp-r / mb-r } or { ng-kr / ng-gr }

SHORT FORMS

character   *wonderful* or *wonderfully*

rather or *writer*   *therefore*   *interest*

Phrases: The doubling principle is used in phrases to add the words *their, there, other,* or *dear:*

in their   *have their*   *I am sure there is*

some other   *my dear sir*   *my dear madam*

Special Phrases: *in order that* *in order to* *rather than*

not later than *no longer than* *this letter*

EXERCISE 125

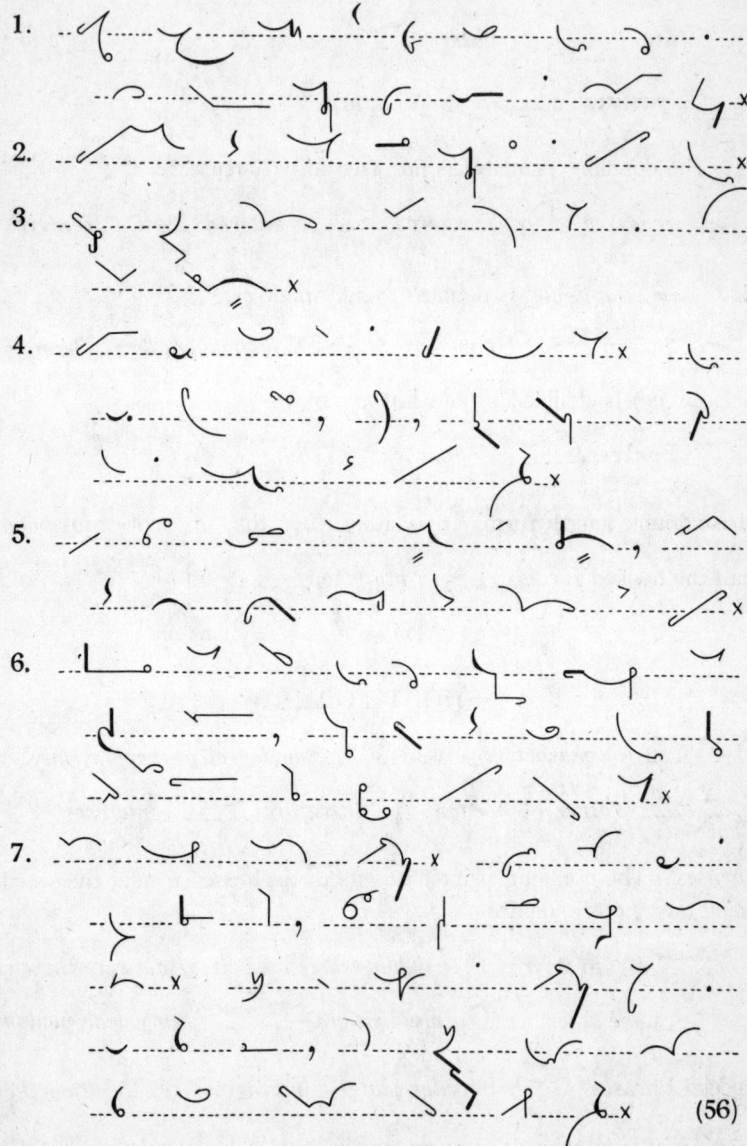

(56)

8.

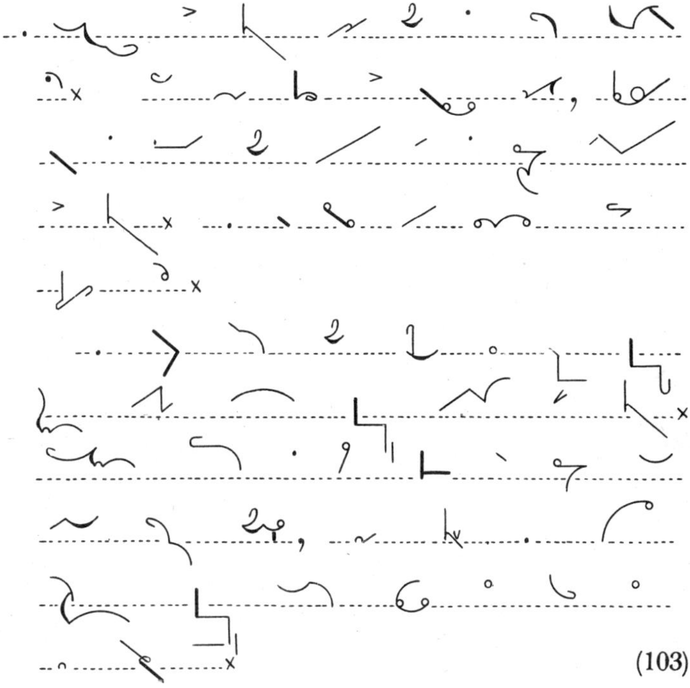

(103)

EXERCISE 126

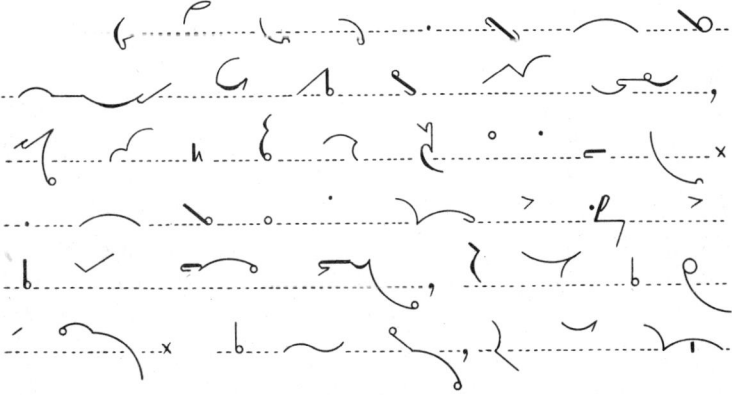

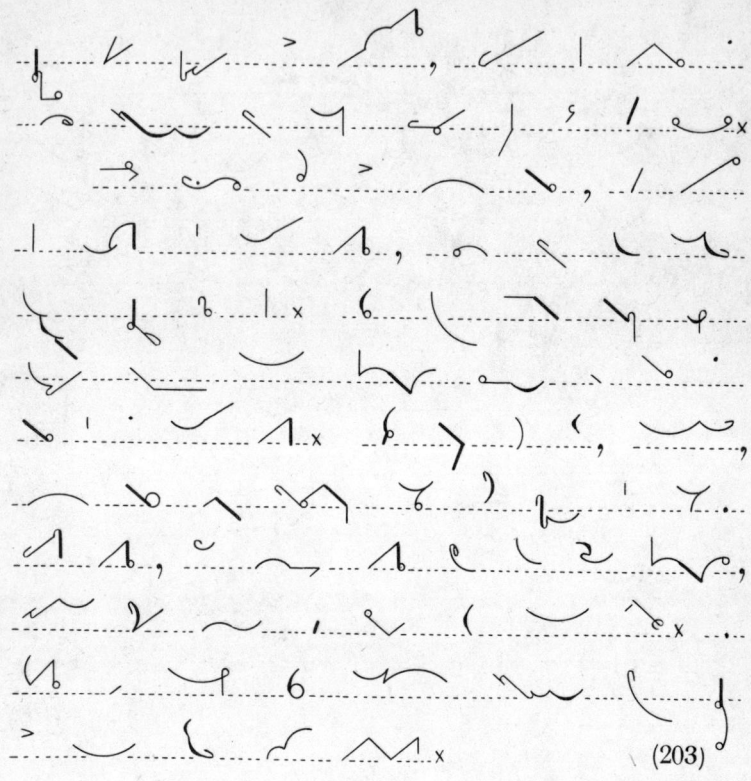

EXERCISE 127

(*Write in Shorthand*)

Mr. Alexander M. Porter, 129 *Third* Avenue, New-York, N. Y.

*My-dear-*Sir: *On behalf of-our-*clients, Messrs. Center *and* Walters, *who-have* requested us *to-represent their* interests *in-the-*matter *of-the* leasehold *on-the building* at 129 *Third* Avenue, *we-wish to* inform-*you that-we-have-their* permission *to* obtain *a* court order, *under-the* terms *of-which you-*will-not-*be-*able-*to* alter *the* front *of-the* building.

We-think-there-is no-doubt *that-the-*terms *of-the* lease *have-been* violated, *and in-our-opinion it-*will-*be to-your* interest *to* halt *any* further operations until *a* decision *has-been* rendered by-*the* court. *Very-*truly-*yours.* (108)

CHAPTER XVI

73. Prefixes

(a) The prefix *con-*, or *com-*, is expressed by a dot, written first at the beginning of an outline, as shown. In words beginning with the *con-* or *com-* dot, the first vowel after the prefix determines the position of the outline:

condition *conduct* *confident* *confidence*

connect *connected* *connection* *consider*

considerable *consideration* *considered* *considering*

contained *consequently* *comfortable* *contents*

continue *continued* *convention* *contract*

concern *concerned* *construction* *conversation*

contrary *company* *committee* *common*

communication *community* *comply* *complete*

completely *complaint*

Special Forms: *commerce* *commission*

(b) *Con-, com, cum-,* or *cog-,* in the middle of a word or phrase is expressed by writing two strokes close to each other:

misconduct *disconnect* *reconsider* *discontinued*

uncommon *discomfort* *circumference* *recognize*

I am confident *you will be compelled*

NEW STANDARD COURSE

74. (*a*) *Accom-* or *accommo-* is expressed by _____ *k*, either joined or disjoined:

⟍⟋ *accomplish* ⟍⟋ *accomplished* ⟋ *accommodate* ⟍ *accompany*

(*b*) *Intro-* is expressed by _____ *ntr:*

⟋ *introduce* ⟋ *introduced*

(*c*) *Magna-*, *magni-*, or *magne-*, is expressed by disjoined *m:*

⟋ *magnanimous* ⟋ *magnificent* ⟋ *magnitude* ⟋ *magnetize*

EXERCISE 128

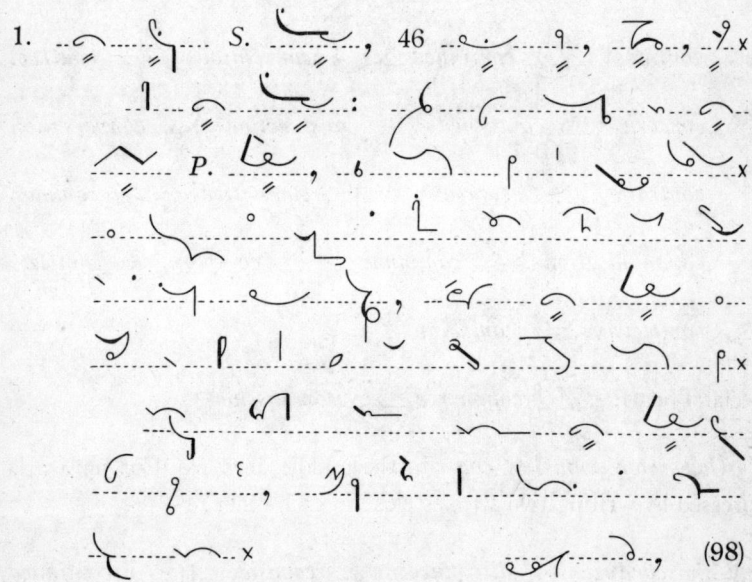

2. 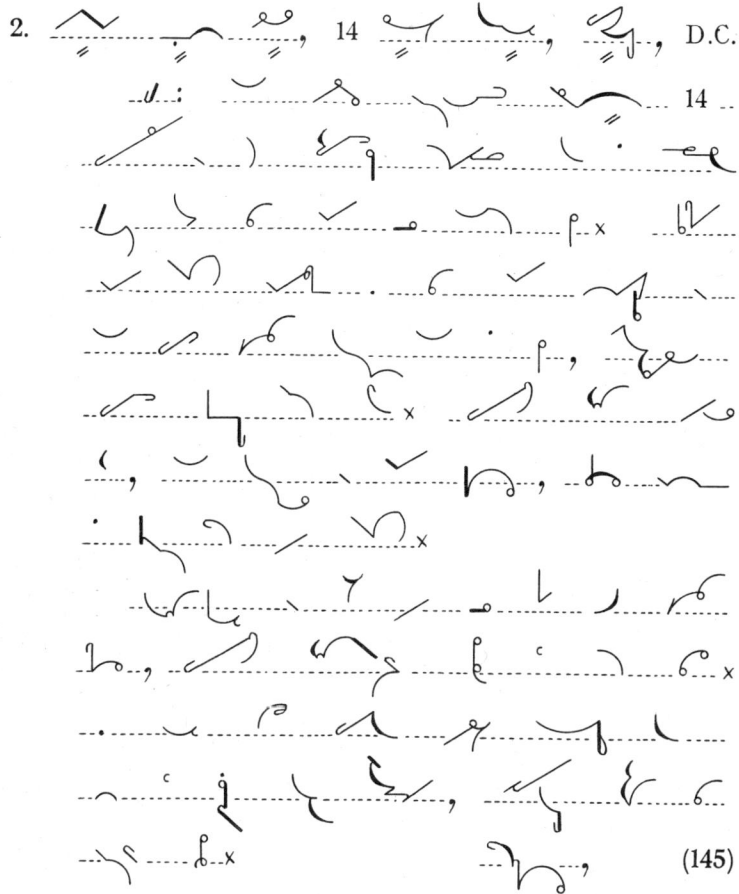 D.C.

(145)

75. (*a*) *Self-* is expressed by a disjoined *s* circle, and *self-con-* is represented by writing the *s* circle in the place of the *con-* dot:

self-defence   self-esteem   self-satisfied

self-contained   self-control

(*b*) *Trans-* may be contracted in most words by omitting the *n*:

transfer   transportation   translate   transcribe

(*c*) *In-* before   str   skr   h (upward) is expressed by a small hook, written in the same direction as the circle:

instruct   instructed   instrument   inscriber

inhabit

(*d*) *Negative Words.* When the prefix *in-* means *not,* it is always expressed by the stroke *n*, as in

inhospitable   inhuman

Other negative words are distinguished from the positive by repeating the first consonant:

known   unknown   necessary   unnecessary

legible   illegible   legal   illegal

SHORT FORMS

commercial-ly   inscribe-d   inscription   instructive

instruction   circumstance   signify-ied-icant

significance

EXERCISE 129

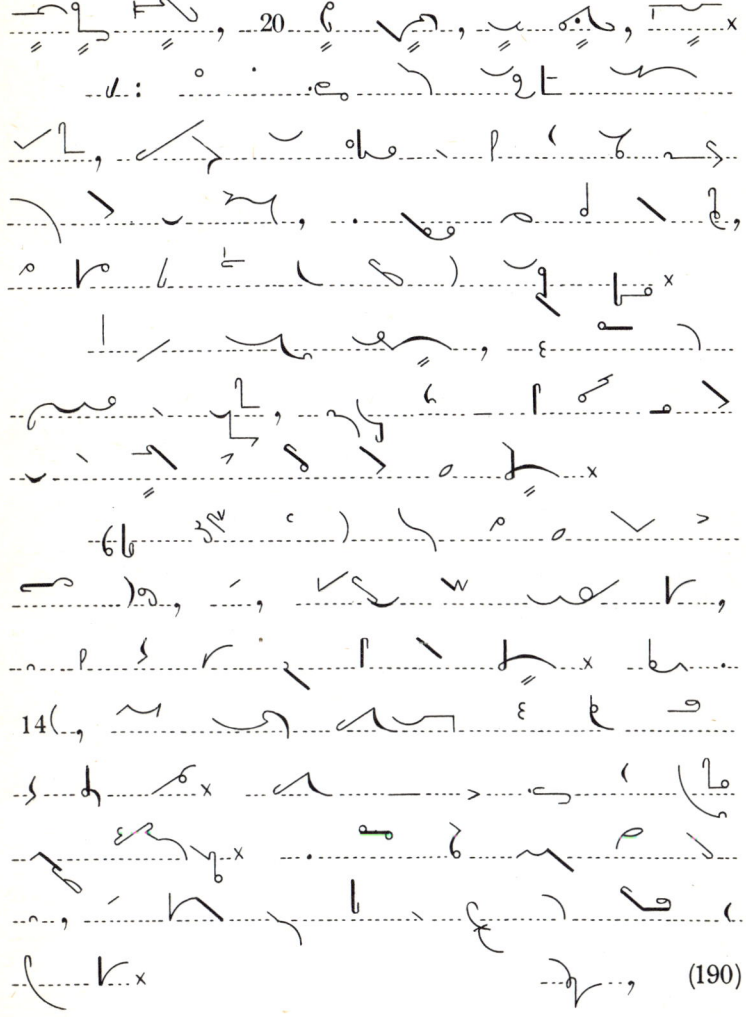

(190)

EXERCISE 130
(Write in Shorthand)

John S. Wilson & Company, *Northern* Avenue, Hartford, Connecticut.

Gentlemen: We-received *your* communication *of-the* 14th, *in-which-you* complain *of-the* delay *in-the* completion *of-your* contract. *That-we-have* failed *to* accomplish *what we*-promised *we*-must admit, *and-we very*-much regret *our* failure.

We-are confident, *however, that-the* contract *could-have-been* completed *as* agreed upon *but for-the* recent trouble *with-the Commercial* Transport Committee, *which-was immediate*ly *responsible for-the* delay. *Their* decision interfered considerably *with our* business, *and-when-we* state *that* only thirty *of-our* transport men *have* continued at work, *we-think-you*-will recognize *how* difficult *it-has-been to* satisfy *our* customers.

It-is-unnecessary *for*-us *to*-add *that-we should* regret-*the* transfer *of-your* business, considering-*the* long connection between us, *and-the* cause *of-the* present interruption. *Very*-truly-*yours,* (139)

76. Suffixes and Word-endings

Where it would be awkward to write ‿ *ng* at the end of a word, the suffix *-ing* is represented by a light dot:

requesting ordering meeting covering serving assisting attempting morning wanting running

The dot *-ing* is used after downward *r* and a light straight downstroke:

securing assuring hearing bearing getting paying teaching eating keeping replying shipping sitting stating staying trying

Usually the dot -*ing* is used after a short form:

⎯. *coming*   ⎯.. *giving*   (*thanking*   (*thinking*   ⎯| *interesting*

Where -*ing* is represented by the dot, the plural -*ings* is represented by a light dash, as shown:

meetings   *mornings*   *hearings*

77. The suffix -*ment* is represented by ⎯ *nt,* where the sign ⎯ *mnt* cannot be easily joined:

achievement   *consignment*   *commencement*   *announcement*

(*a*) The suffix -*mental-ly-ity* is expressed by disjoined *mnt*:

experimental   *departmental*   *sentimental-ly-ity*

(*b*) The endings -*fulness* and -*lessness* are expressed by disjoined *fs,* and *ls* respectively:

thoughtfulness   *thoughtlessness*   *hopefulness*   *hopelessness*

(*c*) The suffix -*ship* is represented by a joined or disjoined *sh*:

friendship   *citizenship*   *hardship*   *membership*   *ownership*

(d) *-Lity* or *-rity*, preceded by any vowel, is expressed by disjoining the preceding stroke:

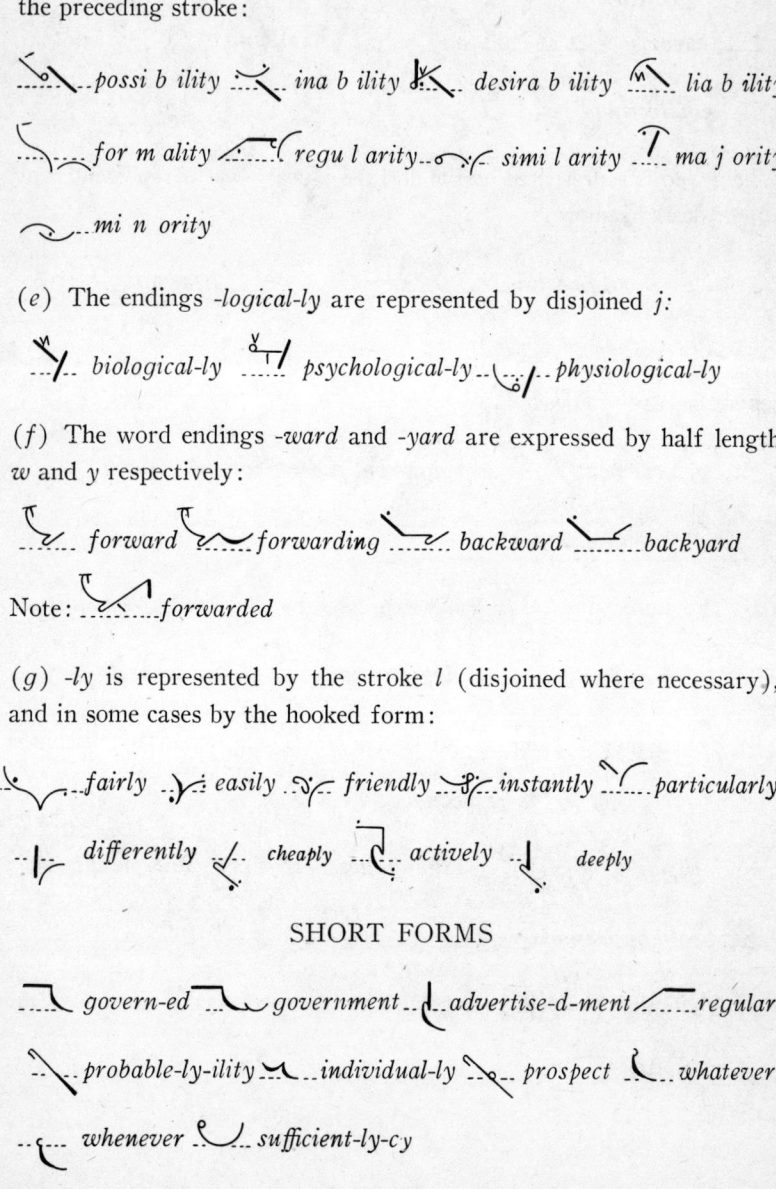

possi b ility   *ina b ility*   *desira b ility*   *lia b ility*

for m ality   *regu l arity*   *simi l arity*   *ma j ority*

mi n ority

(e) The endings *-logical-ly* are represented by disjoined *j*:

biological-ly   *psychological-ly*   *physiological-ly*

(f) The word endings *-ward* and *-yard* are expressed by half length *w* and *y* respectively:

forward   *forwarding*   *backward*   *backyard*

Note: *forwarded*

(g) *-ly* is represented by the stroke *l* (disjoined where necessary), and in some cases by the hooked form:

fairly   *easily*   *friendly*   *instantly*   *particularly*

differently   *cheaply*   *actively*   *deeply*

SHORT FORMS

govern-ed   *government*   *advertise-d-ment*   *regular*

probable-ly-ility   *individual-ly*   *prospect*   *whatever*

whenever   *sufficient-ly-cy*

EXERCISE 131

1.
2.
3. (51)
4. (69)
5. (34)

EXERCISE 132

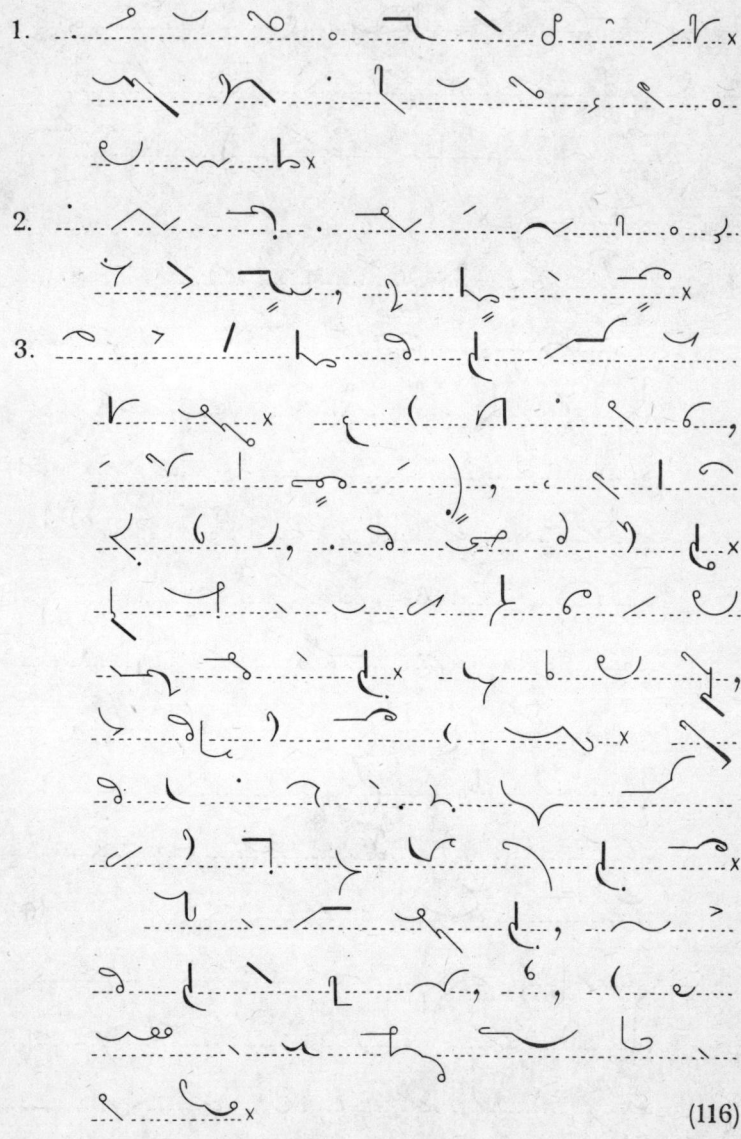

(116)

EXERCISE 133

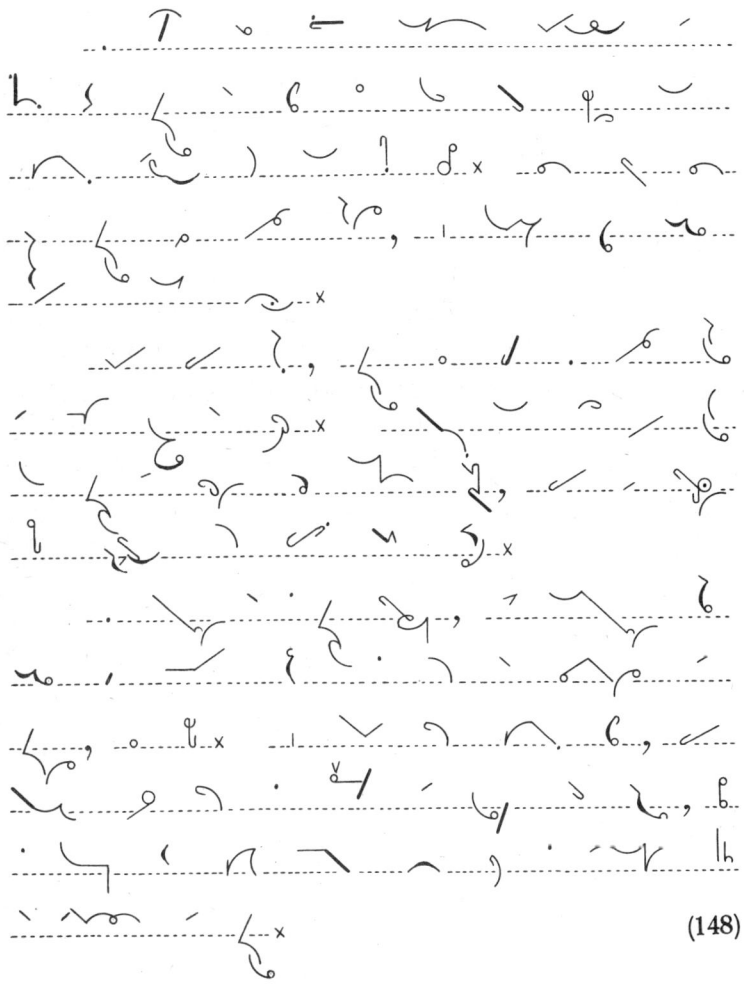

(148)

EXERCISE 134

(*Write in Shorthand*)

Mr. James T. Roberts, 29 Columbus Avenue, Yonkers, New-York.

Dear-Sir: *Your*-letter dated *the* 4th reached us *this* morning. *Your instructions have-been* noted, *but-we-are* afraid *that-it*-will-not-*be* possible *to*-make *all-the* alterations contained *in-your* memorandum *and-have-the* book ready by-*the* end *of-this* month. *However, we* fully recognize-*the* desirability *of-hav*ing-*the publication* completed at *an* early date, *and-we-are* requesting *our* printer *to* hasten-*the* setting *and* printing *as-much-as*-possible.

The inscription will-be-placed after-*the* title page, *as you* desire. Proofs *of-the* last chapters will-*be* forwarded *to-you within a* few days.

Announcements will-*be published in next* Sunday's papers *to-the* effect *that a* new novel by *a* prominent *writer* will *short*ly appear. Please tell-us if-*you would rather have*-us use *your* name *in-the* announcement. *Very*-truly-*yours,* (142)

CHAPTER XVII

78. Diphones

Two consecutive vowels, pronounced in two separate syllables, are represented by the angular signs   These signs are called *Diphones*.

The first represents a dot vowel followed by any other vowel, and the second represents a dash vowel followed by any other vowel. The signs are written in the place of the first vowel of the combination.

(1)   payable   saying   carrying   earlier   earliest   idea   ideal   material   piano   radio   previous   obvious   premium   medium   really   real   realize   convenience   convenient   experience   agreeable   glorious   cordial   courteous   seeing   senior   serious   studying   theater   various

(2)   cooperate   cooperation   following   drawing   growing   knowing   lower   lowest   poem   showing   accruing   jewel

79. The consecutive vowels in words like *question* are represented by the sign   :

  question   union   suggestion   million   guardian

80. Medial *W*

There is a small group of words in which *w* combined with a vowel in the middle of a word is represented by a small semicircle. A left semicircle represents *w* followed by a dot vowel, and a right semicircle represents *w* followed by a dash vowel. The semicircles are written in the place of the vowel with which the *w* is combined:

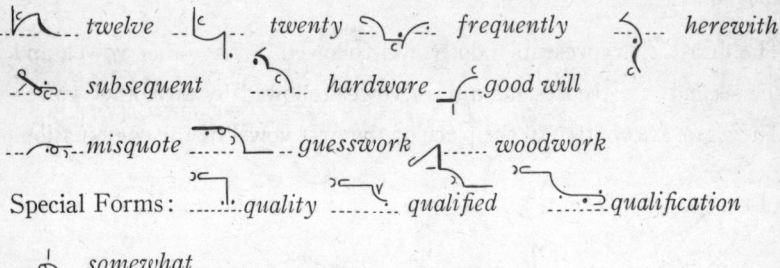

81. Upward *SH*

The stroke ⸺ *sh* is written upward in certain cases to obtain a better outline:

finish, shave, shift, dash, fish, brush, associate, association, appreciate, appreciated, appreciation, foolish, flash, shell, social, shoulder

82. Stroke *R*

In order to keep the outline close to the line of writing, the upward *r* is used where *r* follows two downstrokes, and, for the same reason, downward *r* is used finally after two straight upstrokes:

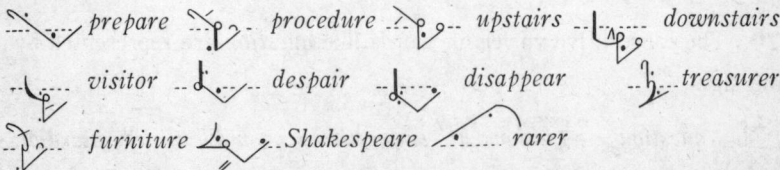

83. Stroke S

The stroke *s* is written (*a*) in words like *science*, *scientific*, *sighing*, *Siam*, where a triphone immediately follows initial *s*, and (*b*) in words like *continuous*, *fatuous*, *strenuous*, *pious*, where the final syllable *-ous* is immediately preceded by a diphthong.

SHORT FORMS

danger   *financial-ly*   *mortgage-d*   *neglect-ed*   *practice-d*   *university*   *English*   *exchange-d*   *familiar-ity*   *telegram*

EXERCISE 135

1. [shorthand outlines] 42,691 ... 21 ... 6 ... (75)

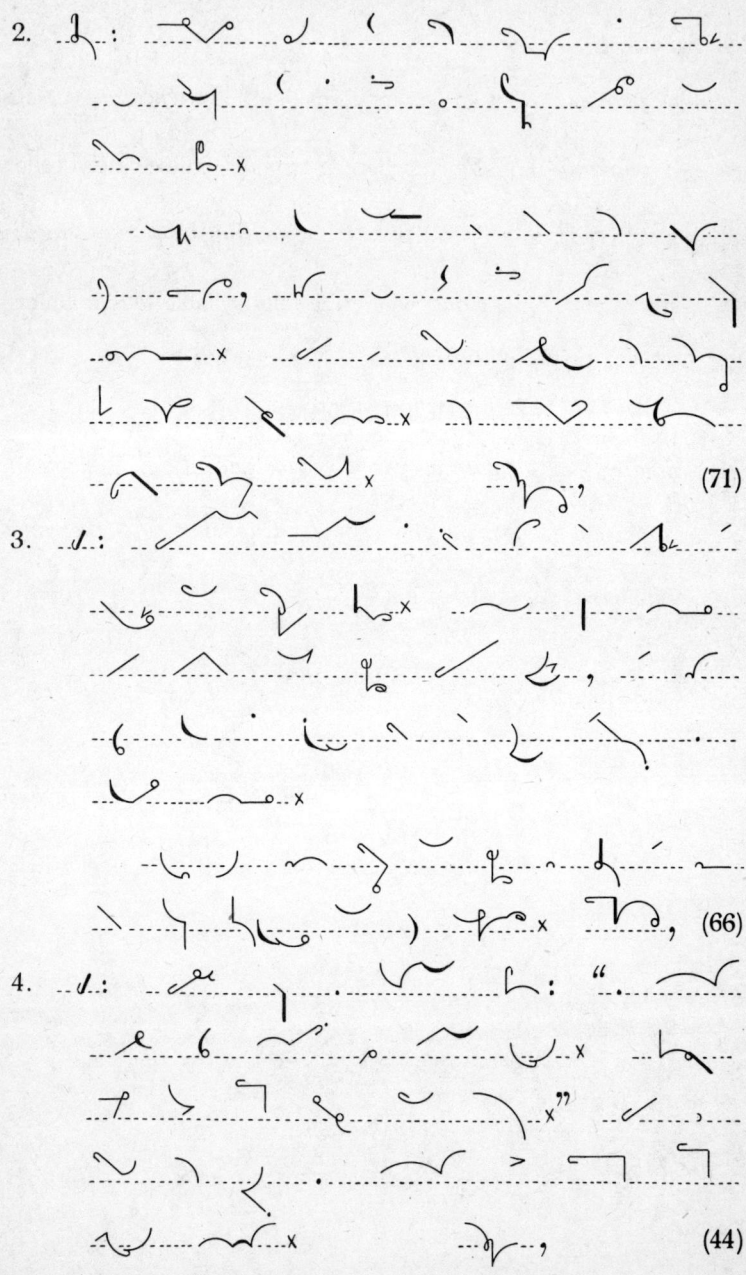

5.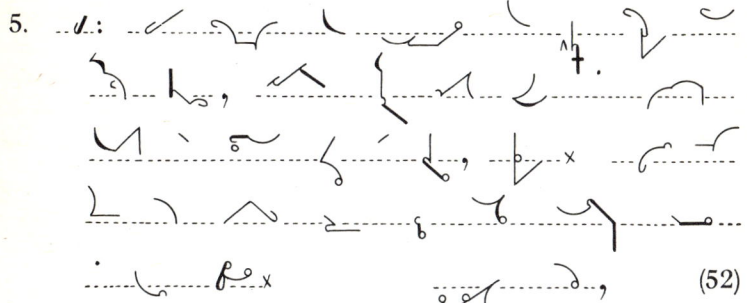

(52)

EXERCISE 136

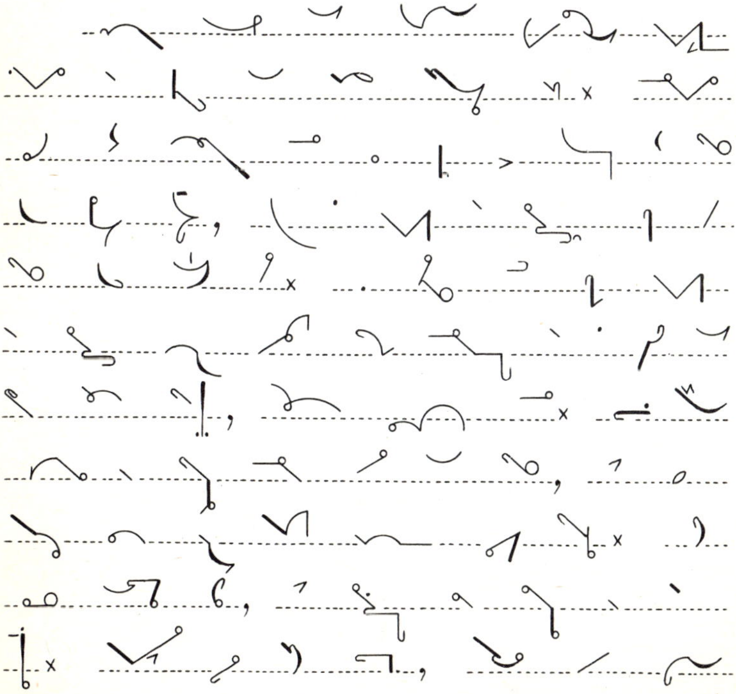

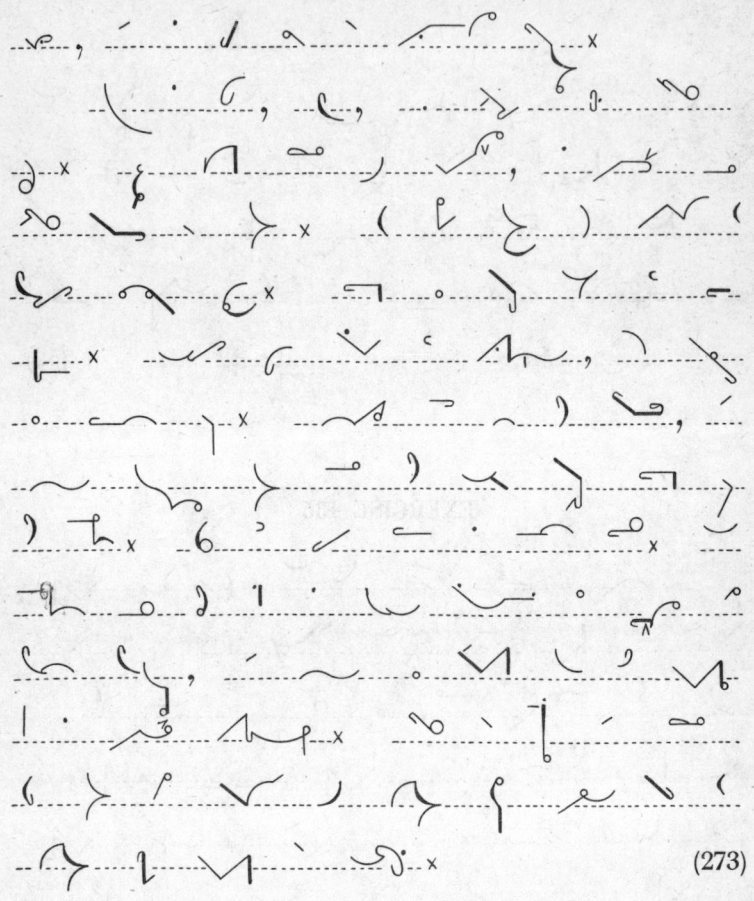

(273)

EXERCISE 137

(Write in Shorthand)

1. William J. Anderson, *who-is a* professor *of English* at Columbia University, *has* recently compiled *a* book *of* quotations *from* Shakespeare. *An* examination *of-the* book shows *that-we-do*-not-*have to-go to-the* theater *to*-hear-*the language of* Shakespeare, *for-we* use *his* terms *and*-phrases constantly *in-our* everyday speech. (53)

2. *We-are* so *familiar with-the*-many conveniences *which* science *has put within our* reach *that-we-do*-not realize or appreciate *the* debt *we owe to* science. Constant use *and familiarity with-the* various time-saving *and* labor-saving devices tend *to*-make-*us over*look *their* tremendous value. *The* contributions *to-our* comfort *and* convenience by men *of* scientific training *are* continuous, *and*-they-*have* made-*the* modern world *a wonderful* place *to*-live *in*. (76)

3. *The* treasurer prepares *a* statement *of-the financial* condition *of-the* company annually. *This* statement *is usually* mailed *to-the* stockholders *in-the* case *of a public* corporation. *A* comparison *with* previous annual reports, or *balance* sheets, shows *whether-the year's trad*ing *has-been more* or less profitable. (48)

4. *It-is-the practice of large insurance* firms *to* invest *the* bulk *of-their* funds *in first mortgages on buildings,* homes, *and* farms. *It-is* considered *that* real estate *is* less liable *to* sudden changes *in* value, *and, therefore, there-is* less *danger of-the* companies *hav*ing *to* suffer *any financial* loss through *a* sudden drop *in-the* value *of-their* holdings. (62)

5. *Dear*-Sir: Will-*you* please consider my application *for-the* position *of*-treasurer *in-your organization. I believe-that I-have-the* necessary qualifications *and* experience, *and-I*-enclose *a* summary *of-them for-your* information. If-*it-is* convenient, *I-shall* appreciate *an opportunity to* discuss my application *with-you, and any* questions *you*-may desire *to* ask *can-be* answered fully *during-the* course *of-our* interview. *Yours-respect*fully, (71)

CHAPTER XVIII
84. Figures

Figures *one* to *seven* and the figure *nine* are best represented by shorthand outlines. Other numbers, except round numbers, are represented by the ordinary Arabic numerals.

Round numbers are represented as follows:

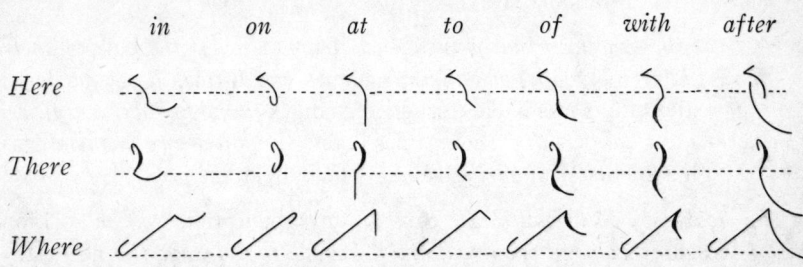

85. Compound Words

Compounds of *here, there, where,* are written as follows:

	in	on	at	to	of	with	after
Here							
There							
Where							

86. Intersections

The practice of intersecting one stroke through another is a very useful device for the representation of very commonly occurring phrases.

The device may be adapted to meet the special needs of the writer. Thus, for some shorthand writers the stroke *p* might usefully represent the word *party*, whereas in an insurance office the stroke *p* might better be used to represent *policy*.

PITMAN SHORTHAND

Where intersection is not practicable, write one stroke close to another. The following list shows how the device may be used:

P	represents	*party*		Democratic Party
				Republican Party
B	"	*bank* or *bill*		bank rate
				city bank
				bill of lading
T	"	*attention*		early attention
				necessary attention
D	"	*department*		science department
				foreign department
CH	"	*charge*		this charge
				free of charge
J	"	*Journal*		Bankers' Journal
				Journal of Commerce
K	"	*company, cover,* or *captain*		this company
				under separate cover
				Captain Thompson
G	"	*government*		government official
				government office

F	represents	*form*		necessary form
				as a matter of form
TH	"	*month*		in a month's time
				for a month
M	"	*manager, morning,* or *mark*		general manager
				Monday morning
				auditor's mark
N	"	*national*		national defence
				national affairs
RAY	"	*require-d-ment railway,* or *railroad*		you may require
				will be required
				your requirements
				Central Railroad
R	"	*arrange-d-ment*		please make arrangements
				we have arranged
Kr	"	*corporation,* or *colonel*		public corporation
				Colonel Alexander
Pr	"	*professor*		Professor Jackson

PITMAN SHORTHAND

SHORT FORMS

inconvenience-t-ly   distinguish-ed   income   become

becoming   welcome   nevertheless

EXERCISE 138

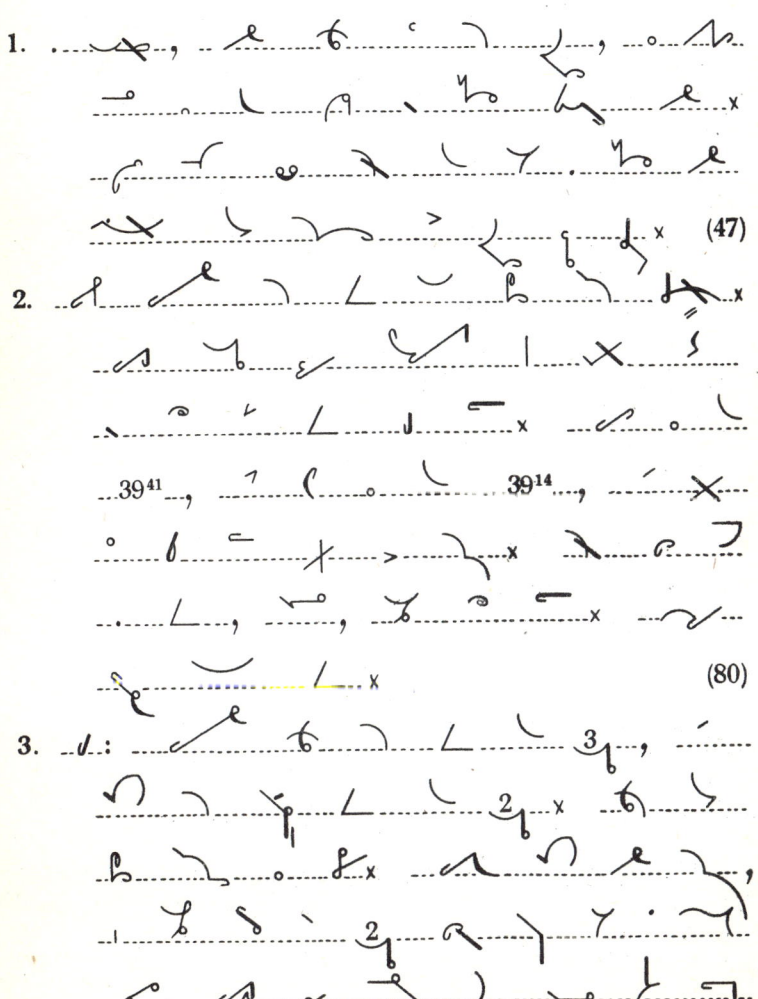

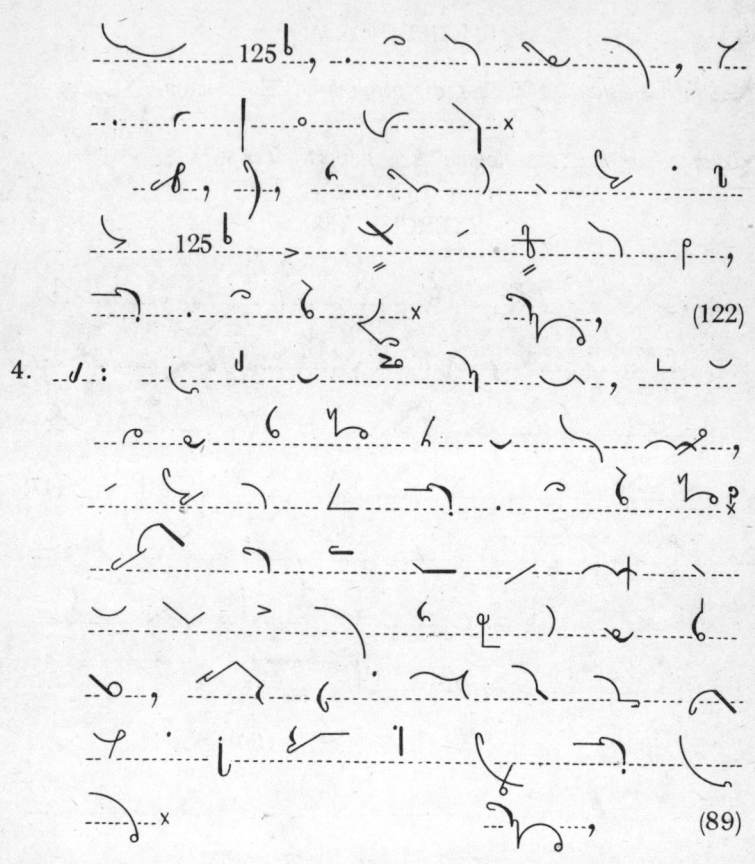

EXERCISE 139

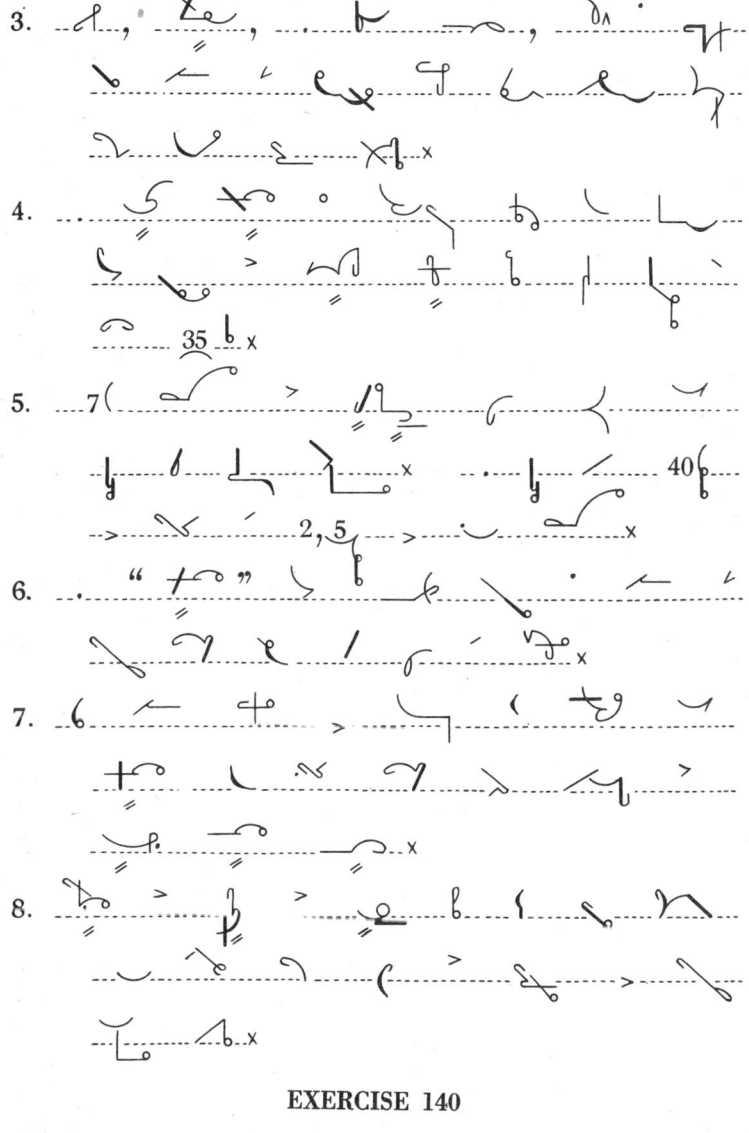

EXERCISE 140

149(...

_13_... (74)

2. ...

(108)

3. ...

(54)

APPENDIX

Principal Cities

New York
Chicago (Ill.)
Philadelphia (Pa.)
Detroit (Mich.)
Los Angeles (Calif.)
Cleveland (Ohio)
St. Louis (Mo.)
Baltimore (Md.)
Boston (Mass.)
Pittsburgh (Pa.)
San Francisco (Calif.)
Buffalo (N. Y.)
Milwaukee (Wis.)
Washington (D. C.)
New Orleans (La.)
Minneapolis (Minn.)
Cincinnati (Ohio)
Newark (N. J.)
Kansas City (Mo.)
Indianapolis (Ind.)
Seattle (Wash.)
Atlanta (Ga.)
Rochester (N. Y.)
Jersey City (N. J.)
Louisville (Ky.)
Portland (Ore.)

Denver (Colo.)
Houston (Texas)
Toledo (Ohio)
Oakland (Calif.)
Columbus (Ohio)
St. Paul (Minn.)
Dallas (Texas)
Birmingham (Ala.)
Akron (Ohio)
San Antonio (Texas)
Memphis (Tenn.)
Providence (R. I.)
Omaha (Nebr.)
Syracuse (N. Y.)
Dayton (Ohio)
Worcester (Mass.)
Oklahoma City (Okla.)
Youngstown (Ohio)
Grand Rapids (Mich.)
Fort Worth (Texas)
New Haven (Conn.)
    or
Hartford (Conn.)
Hollywood (Calif.)
Nashville (Tenn.)

States and Territories

Alabama	Missouri
Alaska	Montana
Arizona	Nebraska
Arkansas	Nevada
California	New Hampshire
Canal Zone	New Jersey
Colorado	New Mexico
Connecticut	New York
Delaware	North Carolina
District of Columbia	North Dakota
	Ohio
Florida	Oklahoma
Georgia	Oregon
Idaho	Pennsylvania
Illinois	Rhode Island
Indiana	South Carolina
Iowa	South Dakota
Kansas	Tennessee
Kentucky	Texas
Louisiana	Utah
Maine	Vermont
Maryland	Virginia
Massachusetts	Washington
Michigan	West Virginia
Minnesota	Wisconsin
Mississippi	Wyoming

Short Forms

Arranged alphabetically

The number in parenthesis indicates the Chapter in which the word is presented.

A

- a (4)
- accord-ing (14)
- acknowledge (15)
- advantage (12)
- advertise-ment-d (16)
- all (9)
- altogether (10)
- an (4)
- and (6)
- any (5)
- anything (9)
- are (6)
- as (8)
- as is (9)

B

- balance (12)
- balanced (12)
- be (1)
- because (8)
- become (18)
- been (12)
- behalf (12)
- belief (11)
- believe-d (11)
- beyond (7)
- build-ing (11)
- but (1)

C

- call (11)
- called (11)
- can (5)
- cannot (12)
- care (11)
- cared (14)
- certificate (15)
- character (15)
- circumstance (16)
- cold (11)
- come (3)
- commercial-ly (16)
- could (10)

D

- danger (17)
- dear (11)
- deliver-y-ed (11)
- description (11)
- different-ce (5)
- difficult (12)
- difficulty (12)
- distinguish-ed (18)
- do (1)
- doctor, Dr. (11)
- dollar (4)
- during (11)

E

- English (17)
- equal-ly (11)
- equaled (11)
- especial-ly (9)
- everything (11)
- exchange-d (17)
- expect-ed (10)
- eye (7)

F

- familiar-ity (17)
- February (10)
- financial-ly (17)
- first (9)
- for (4)

from (11)

G

general-ly (12)
gentleman (12)
gentlemen (12)
give-n (3)
go (5)
gold (12)
govern-ed (16)
govern-
  ment (16)
great (12)
guard (12)

H

had (4)
hand (15)
has (8)
have (2)
he (7)
him (3)
himself (9)
his (8)
hour (6)
how (7)
however (11)

I

I (7)
immediate (15)
important-
  -ce (14)
impossible (14)
improve-d-
  -ment (14)
in (5)
income (18)
inconvenience-
  -t-ly (18)
individual-
  -ly (16)
influence (9)
influenced (9)
inform-ed (10)
informa-
  tion (13)
inscribe-d (16)
inscription (16)
inspect-ed-
  -ion (10)
instruction (16)
instructive (16)
insurance (10)
interest (15)
investiga-
  tion (13)
is (8)
is as (9)
it (1)
itself (9)

J

January (10)

K

knowledge (15)

L

language (9)
large (6)
largely (11)
larger (11)
largest (9)
liberty (11)

M

me (7)
member (11)
mere (11)
more (11)
mortgage-d
  (17)
most (9)
Mr. (11)
much (9)
myself (9)

N

near (11)
neglect-ed (17)
never (10)
neverthe-
  less (18)
New York (9)
next (9)
nor (11)
northern (12)
nothing (9)
November (10)
number-ed (11)

O

- object-ed (13)
- objection (13)
- of (4)
- on (4)
- opinion (12)
- opportu-nity (14)
- organiza-tion (13)
- organize-d (13)
- ought (5)
- our (6)
- ourselves (9)
- over (11)
- owe (5)
- owing (9)
- own (11)
- owner (11)

P

- particular (14)
- people (11)
- pleasure (11)
- practice-d (17)
- principal--ly (11)
- principle (11)
- probable--ly-ility (16)
- prospect (16)
- public (13)
- publication (13)
- publish-ed (13)
- put (5)

Q

- quite (10)

R

- rather (15)
- regular (16)
- remark-ed (11)
- remember--ed (11)
- represent--ed (12)
- represen-tative (12)
- respect-ed (10)
- respectful--ly (11)
- responsi-ble-ility (12)

S

- satisfaction (13)
- satisfactory (10)
- school (15)
- schooled (15)
- sent (10)
- several (8)
- shall (2)
- short (15)
- should (6)
- significance (16)
- significant (16)
- signify-ied (16)
- something (9)
- southern (12)
- speak (8)
- special-ly (8)
- spirit (15)
- subject-ed (8)
- sufficient--ly-cy (16)
- sure (11)
- surprise (11)
- surprised (11)

T

- telegram (17)
- tell (11)
- thank-ed (6)
- that (10)
- the (1)
- their (11)
- them (2)
- themselves (9)
- there (11)
- therefore (15)
- thing (3)
- think (2)
- third (12)
- this (8)
- those (8)
- though (9)
- thus (8)
- till (11)

to (1)	V	wished (10)
to be (5)	very (11)	with (7)
together (10)	W	within (12)
told (12)		without (10)
too (1)	was (2)	wonderful-ly (15)
toward (12)	we (3)	
trade (12)	welcome (18)	word (15)
tried (12)	what (7)	would (7)
truth (11)	whatever (16)	writer (15)
two (1)	when (7)	
	whenever (16)	Y
U	whether (14)	yard (15)
under (15)	which (1)	year (6)
United States (9)	who (1)	you (7)
university (17)	whose (6)	young (9)
usual-ly (2)	why (7)	your (6)
	wish (5)	yesterday (13)

Contractions
LIST ONE

The Short Forms given in the text are for words included in lists of the two thousand commonest words, and are therefore very frequently used. The following additional contractions will be found useful in high-speed writing. The words occur in lists of the ten thousand commonest words.

A

administration
administrative
administrator
appointment
arbitrary
arbitration
architect-ure-al
assignment

B

bankruptcy

C

capable
characteristic
contentment

D

dangerous
defective
deficient-ly-cy
democracy-atic
demonstrate
demonstration

E

destruction
discharge-d

E

efficient-ly-cy
electric
electrical
electricity
emergency
England
enlarge
enlargement
entertainment
enthusiastic-m
establish-ed-ment
executive
executor
expediency
expenditure
expensive

I

identical
identification
imperfect-ion-ly

incorporated
independent-ly-ce
indispensable-ly
influential-ly
intelligence
intelligent-ly
introduction
investment
irregular

J

jurisdiction
justification

L

legislative
legislature

M

manufacture-d
manufacturer
manuscript
mathematics
maximum
mechanical-ly
messenger
minimum
ministry
misfortune
monstrous

N

negligence
notwithstanding

O

objectionable
objective

P

passenger
peculiar-ity
perform-ed
performance
practicable
prejudice-d-ial-ly
preliminary
production
productive
project-ed
proportion-ed
prospective
publisher

Q

questionable-ly

R

reform-ed
remarkable-ly
representation
republic
republican

respective
respectively

S

selfish-ness
sensible-ly-ility
stranger

subscribe-d
subscription
substantial-ly
suspect-ed
sympathetic

T

telegraphic
thankful

U

unanimous-ly
uniform-ity-ly
universal
universe

V

valuation

Contractions
LIST TWO

(These words do not occur in lists of the ten thousand commonest words.)

A

abandonment
administrate
administratrix
amalgamate
amalgamation
arbitrate
arbitrator
attainment

C

circumstantial
contingency
cross-examination
cross-examine-d

D

denomination-al
destructive
destructively

E

enlarger
enlightenment
executrix
exigency
extinguish-ed

F

falsification
familiarization
familiarize

G

generalization

H

henceforward
howsoever

I

imperturbable
inconsiderate
informer
intelligible-ly
irrecoverable-ly
irremovable-ly
irrespective
irrespectively
irresponsible-ility

M

magnetic-ism
mathematical-ly
mathematician

metropolitan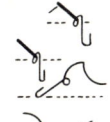

O

obstruction
obstructive
oneself
organizer

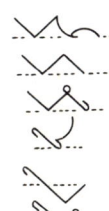

P

performer
perpendicular
perspective
proficient-ly-cy
proportionate-ly
prospectus

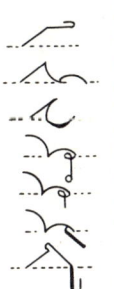

R

recoverable
reformer
relinquish-ed
remonstrance
remonstrate
removable
reproduction

retrospect
retrospection
retrospective

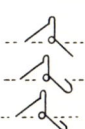

S

signification
stringency
subjection
subjective

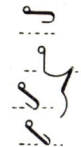

T

thenceforward

U

unanimity
universality
unprincipled

W

whensoever
whereinsoever
wheresoever
whithersoever

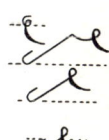

INDEX

The figures refer to the **paragraphs,** *except where the page is mentioned.*

A

Abbreviated *W*, 37
Accom-, Prefix, 74
Additional Forms—Double Consonants, 42, 43, 44, 45
Appendix, Pages 171-183

C

Capitals, 2
Circle *S*, 21, 22, 23, 24
Circle *S* and Double Consonants, 38, 40
Circle *S* and *N* and *F* hooks, 50, 51
Circle *S* and *L*, 27
Circle *S* and Phrasing, 23
Circle *SES*, 30
Circle *SW*, 31
Cities, Outlines for Names of, Page 173
Compound Consonants, 60
Compound Words, 85
Con-, com-, cum-, cog-, Prefixes, 73
Consonants, 1, 8, 10, 14, 15, 16, 20
Consonants, Compound, 60
Consonants, Double—Curves, 42
Consonants, Double—Straight Strokes, 38, 39
Consonant *H*, 20, 62
Consonants, Joining of, 3
Consonants, Omission of, 63
Contractions, 63
Contractions, Additional List of, Pages 179, 182

D

D Indicated by Halving, 33, 34
Diphones, 78

Diphthongs, 17, 18
Diphthongs and Halving, 34
Dr Indicated by Doubling, 68
Double Consonants, Additional Forms, 42, 43, 44, 45
Double Consonants and *S* Circle, 38, 40
Double Consonants—Curves, 42
Double Consonants—Special Use of, 41
Double Consonants, Straight Strokes, 38, 39
Doubling Principle, 68, 69, 70, 71, 72
Doubling Principle and Phrasing, 72
Downward *L*, 27, 36

F

F and *N* Hooks and *S* Circle, 50, 51
F and *N* Hooks, medially, 49
Figures, 84
First-Place Vowels, 11
First Position, 11
Fl, Vl, Additional Signs for, 43
F or *V* Hook, 47
Fr, Vr, etc., Additional Signs for, 42
-fulness—Word-ending, 77

G

Gr added to *Ng*, 45

H

Halving, 33, 34, 35, 59, 64
Halving—Disjoined *t* or *d*, 67
Halving—Finally Hooked Strokes, **48**
Halving, Not used, 35
Halving—Phrasing, 67
Halving— *-Shun* Hook, 59
H Consonant, 20, 62

I

In-, Prefix, 75
-ing, Suffix, 76
Intersections, 86
Intro-, Prefix, 74

K

Kr Added to *ng*, 45

L

L and Phrasing, 10
L and the Circle, 27
L Downward, 27, 36
-lessness—Word-ending, 77
-lity, 77
-logical-ly, 77
Loop *St*, 28
Loop *Str*, 29
-ly, Suffix, 77

M

Magna-, Magni-, Magne-, 74
-ment, 77
-mental-ly-ity, 77
Mp, Mb Doubled, 72

N

N and *F* Hooks and *S* Circle, 50, 51
N and *F* Hooks, Medially, 49
-nce, 53
Negative Words, 75
N Hook, 46
Ng Doubled to Add *kr* or *gr*, 72
Ng Hooked to Add *kr* or *gr*, 45

P

Phrasing Defined, 6
Phrasing—Doubling Principle, 72
Phrasing—Diphthongs, 18
Phrasing—Halving Principle, 67
Phrasing—*L*, 10
Phrasing—*S* Circle, 23
Phrasing—Stroke *H*, 20
Phrasing—*SW* Circle, 31
Pl Series, 38
Position, First, 11
Position, Second, 12
Position, Third, 13
Position of Half Length Strokes, 34
Pr Series, 39
Prefixes, 73, 74, 75
Punctuation, 7

R

R, Two Forms for, 14, 15, 16, 26, 82
-rity, 77

S

S Circle, 21, 22, 23, 24, 38, 40, 50, 51
S Circle and Phrasing, 23
Second-Place Vowels, 2, 4, 9
Second Position, 12
Self-, Prefix, 75
Self-con-, Prefix, 75
Ses Circle, 30
Short Forms, Alphabetically Arranged, Page 175
Short Forms Defined, 5
-ship, Suffix, 77
Shr and *Shl*, How Written, 44
-shun Hook, 55, 56, 57, 58, 59
Sh Upward, 81
Special Use of Double Consonants, 41
States, Outlines for Names of, Page 174
St Loop, 28
Str Loop, 29
Strokes *S* and *Z*, When Used, 32, 83
Stroke *Z*, 25
Suffixes and Word-endings, 76, 77
Sw Circle 31

T

Third-Place Vowels, 13
Third Position, 13
Tick *The,* 6
T Indicated by Halving, 33, 34
THr Indicated by Doubling, 68
Trans-, Prefix, 75
Tr, Dr, or *THr,* Indicated by Doubling, 68
Triphones, 19
-ture, Indicated by Doubling, 70

V

Vowel *aw* Joined Initially, 28
Vowel Indication, 14, 15, 32, 35, 36, 54, 57, 66
Vowels Before and After Strokes, 2, 10
Vowels Between Two Strokes, 13
Vowels, First-Place, 11
Vowels, Second-Place, 2, 4, 9
Vowels, Third-Place, 13

W

W Abbreviated, 37
-ward—Word-ending, 77
Whl, 61
Wl, 61
W—Medial Semicircle, 80

Y

-yard, Word-ending, 77

Z

Z at the Beginning, 25